BIKE TRIBES

A Field Guide to North American Cyclists

Bicycling

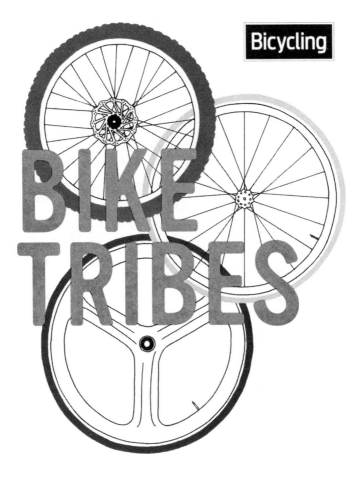

BIKE TRIBES

Mike Magnuson
Illustrations by Danica Novgorodoff

RODALE.

Rodale books may be purchased for business or promotional use or for special sales. For information, please write to: Special Markets Department, Rodale Inc., 733 Third Avenue, New York, NY 10017.

Printed in the United States of America

Rodale Inc. makes every effort to use acid-free ♾, recycled paper ♻.

Book design by Kara Plikaitis

Illustrations by Danica Novgorodoff

Library of Congress Cataloging-in-Publication Data

Magnuson, Mike, 1963–
  Bike tribes : a field guide to North American cyclists / Mike Magnuson ; illustrations by Danica Novgorodoff.
     p.   cm.
  ISBN 978-1-60961-743-1   hardcover
  1. Cyclists—North America.   2. Cycling—North America.   3. Athletic clubs—North America.   I. Title.
GV1046.N8M34   2012
796.6097—dc23

2011049891

Distributed to the trade by Macmillan

2   4   6   8   10   9   7   5   3   1   hardcover

We inspire and enable people to improve their lives and the world around them.
www.rodalebooks.com

ACKNOWLEDGMENTS

First and foremost, thanks so much to Shannon Welch, Kara Plikaitis, and Marie Croussilat at Rodale. I appreciate the positive vibe and good humor throughout this very cool project.

Special thanks, of course, to the amazing Danica Novgorodoff, artist of the highest order. When our book team goes for a ride, you will for sure drop us like a bad memory! Or will that be Kara dropping everybody? The whole team agrees, in any event, that I will be off the back and that Shannon will be calling the shots.

I would also like to thank my friends at *Bicycling* magazine, particularly Bill Strickland, Dave Howard, and Peter Flax. I owe you guys bigtime for putting up with me all these years, even when my rubber hasn't been able to meet the road in the time allotted. One thing's for sure: We have always done so much more than write pieces about bikes.

Thanks to Scott Bicycles and Trek Bicycles and Rocky Mountain Bicycles, whose bikes I have had the privilege of riding hither and yon over the last couple of years.

Thanks, too, to my longtime literary agent, Lisa Bankoff, who has made a continuing life in words possible for me.

Additional thanks to the Pacific University MFA Program in Creative Writing, for giving me the opportunity to teach in such a wonderful writing environment; thanks to my sister Sandy, who is my loyal friend no matter what; and thanks to Sue Curtis Wellnitz, who never tires of talking and laughing about nothing in particular and who is 100 percent awesome 100 percent of the time.

Last, and most assuredly not least, I would like to thank the following cyclists who filled out extensive survey material that served as the foundation for the stories in this book: Mike Ahrens, Stephanie Hill Alexander, John Alltop, Dale Aschemann, David Barnas, Roberto Barrios, Scott Baste, Gerald Beam, David Beriss, Darla Biel, Alan Brown, Nancy Brown, Mike Busch, Pete Butler, Wesley Cheney, Mike Clark, Fred Crawford, Brendan Collier, Jessica Conner, Ken Coonley, Robert Costin, Rebecca Davis, Bruce Dickman, Thomas Durkin, Justin Evans, Maggie Eytalis, Chandra Gallipeau, David Gill, Lara Goodman, Jonathan Gray, Carina Hahn, Jason Harrod, Jenny Oh Hatfield, Kyle Hollasch, Andrew Homan, Ed Huntley, Samuel Janes, Avalon Jenkins, Scott Johnson, Eddie Jones, Amy King, Katie Kingsbury, Ken Kubiak, Amanda LaClaire, Beth Leasure, Joe Linton, Don Lowe, Robin Lowe, Lorri Lee Lown, Jon Mason, Monique Pua Mata, Louis Messina, Ellen Michaelson, Benjamin Miller, Paul Mollway, Alison Moore, David Neis, Kevin O'Dowd, David Peterson, Lou Plummer, John Pyeatt, John Reimbold, Kevin Remington, Andrea Richardson, Anne Rock, Mark Rhode, Dulcy Rojas, Flavia Sancier, Heather Sappenfield, Darren Sherkat, Marla Shock-Stephens, Kim Solano, Chris Strout, Mark Swartzendruber, Chris Thomas, Heidi Van Beek, Kelley Walker, Jeff Williams, Paul Wood, and Michele Zebrowitz.

This book is for the Heckawee:

Executive Counsel Dale Aschemann, Roberto "Bob" Barrios,
Big Tom Harbert, Michael "Molteni" Humphries,
David "Champ" Neis, Mike "Napoleon" Pease, John "Chief" Reimbold,
and Professor Darren Sherkat.

May we forever not care how long it takes us to get there or how much Cave Creek we may drink along the way.

CONTENTS

1 We Shall Call Them Bike Tribes

7 Minding the Store

17 The Wrench Who Keeps Us Rolling

27 BMX

33 The Overwhelming Majority

43 The Occasionally Dirty

51 The Shrinking People

61 One Part of Three Parts

77 Riders of the Century

89 Thousands upon Thousands of Us

97 The Mothers of All Centuries

105 Roadies

123 Those Who Chase Each Other in the Woods

133 When in Doubt, Cyclocross

143 The Legend of Rando

149 The Happy Wanderers

155 The Commuters

169 The Mass Is Critical

175 We Can Fixie This

187 What Vintage Do You Prefer?

193 Beach Cruisers

197 Together

199 Acknowledgments

WE SHALL CALL THEM
BIKE TRIBES

Sometimes the hardest things to understand are the easiest to explain. Like breathing. That's easy enough to explain. If we stop breathing and don't start breathing again in a jiffy, we'll die. Little kids can understand that. Little kids can easily understand sunshine and green plants and where oxygen comes from, too. Their teachers have explained how the sun strikes the leaves and feeds the plants and the plants in turn feed us and how, when plants breathe, they make oxygen for us. Without sunshine, all little kids know, there would be no life at all.

But how do plants breathe anyway? How can plants *eat* sunshine when human beings are getting *burned* by it? And why do schoolteachers say if we stare at the sun we'll go blind? Little kids will blow their minds on the spot if they think about that sort of stuff too long. Same is true of grown-ups. There's just so much we don't know. In fact, I'll bet probably fewer than one person in a thousand can explain, in accurate detail, the actual chemical process of human breathing, *respiration*—the way oxygen passes from our lungs into our bloodstream and makes us strong of body and of mind and of spirit and yet still crazy enough to ride bicycles with our friends 25 miles on the back roads to the next town to buy a Snickers bar and then ride the 25 miles back home. Because that's what respiration does, right? Makes us want to ride bicycles? And is that what's known as the Krebs cycle?

Forgive me. For one thing, I'm obviously not a scientist. For another thing, I'm a lifelong cyclist and somehow have developed an involuntary habit of twisting all avenues of inquiry toward cycling. There *are* scientists who are cyclists, of course, as there are cyclists from every conceivable walk of life. I've known filthy rich cyclists with garages full of bikes, and I've known cyclists who were unemployed and flat broke and begging other cyclists for spare inner tubes and a new chain and a couple of extra energy gels to tide them over till they can catch a break. Some of the cyclists I've known have been brilliant, some not so brilliant. Some of them have been the nicest, most interesting people I've ever met. Some have been total jackasses in every possible connotation of the word. I have been a jackass from time to time, too. I admit it.

Being a jackass is not unique in cycling. Ask any cyclists you know. They'll say the same thing. We have nice people in cycling and mean people and middle-of-the-road people. We have every personality type you can imagine. What cyclists share, incontrovertibly, is this: Deep down, we wouldn't be happy without cycling. In this sense, we are all the same.

○━○━○━○━○━○━○━○━○━○━○━○━○━○━○━○━○━○━○

SO THIS IS a book about people who ride bicycles. I wish it were a book about bicycles without the people attached to them, to tell you the truth, because bicycles are not the most complicated things on this earth, at least compared to human beings, which are unbelievably complicated according to anyone who's ever had anything to say on the matter.

I'm not necessarily an authority on people, either, other than I'm 49 years old and am foolish enough, and proud enough, to believe that age adds up to wisdom. Some days, I'm not sure it does—like when I've forgotten my list at the grocery store for the third time in a row or when I can't remember my own phone number (and who calls themselves anyway?) or get hopelessly lost on a bike ride in the countryside. But not even the wisest soul is wise 100 percent of the time. I've seen some things over the years, I guess, and like most people my age, I've spent considerable periods of my life trying to understand why people think the things they do and why they do the things they do. My general conclusion about people is not very encouraging, but whenever I lay it out there for discussion, I receive support for it. Here's what I believe: People are difficult. That's just a fact everyone agrees on. The other fact people agree on is that no human being, ever, anywhere, has figured out exactly why people are so difficult.

But bicycles are just bikes. What could bikes possibly do wrong? What could bikes possibly say to offend you? Or misinterpret what you said?

In the most general sense, a cheap bicycle for sale at a department store chain is essentially the same machine as a fancy carbon-fiber road-racing bicycle that you might see in a Pro Tour cycling event. The fancy bike and the cheap bike both have two wheels, a frame, a fork, a crank, pedals, a chain, a seat post, a saddle, and a handlebar. They both smell like rubber and grease when they're new. There is some relatively complicated engineering associated with even the simplest bicycle, for sure, and with a Pro Tour bicycle there is some profoundly complicated aerospace-style engineering involved. But these differences in engineering are salted-in-the-shell peanuts compared with the intricacies of people who pedal these machines. I say this with nearly complete ignorance of engineering, mind you, and with only the fanatical belief that human

3

beings are always more interesting and important than machines. Not all cyclists, it goes without saying, agree with me on this.

But even a dog, the sworn enemy of cyclists since the invention of the bicycle, can wrap its mind around this kind of math: Bicycles + People = Cycling. This means that understanding cyclists should be easy, but the hard truth about cyclists is that very few of us understand each other.

This is how the misunderstanding happens: Millions of people are involved in cycling worldwide. Some ride bikes for transportation. Some ride for exercise and fresh air. Some ride for competition, racing bikes on the road or on the track or on trails or in fields of mud or across the United States or on a long loop around France every July. Some people are as dependent on their bicycle as a heroin addict is on heroin. Some people ride their bicycle one time a year and think that's enough. In general, cycling itself is a highly individual, highly idiosyncratic activity—the type of sport where people quite regularly get into it by riding alone and without having to submit to the greater will of a group. And as a consequence, the people who are drawn to cycling seem to be spirits who follow their own advice, their own guidance, their own ways of thinking about the world and how they ought to be riding bicycles in it.

Nevertheless, for very human reasons, because we don't want to be alone, cyclists tend to gravitate toward other cyclists with whom they feel the highest degree of "alikeness." People who race mountain bikes hang out with other people who race mountain bikes. People who ride bikes for fun hang out with people who ride for fun. It's a matter of group self-selection. Once cyclists become comfortable in their groups, they identify with these groups to the point where they occasionally think things like *This is the way we do it. That means this is the only way to do it.* Once cyclists think things like that, it becomes harder for them to appreciate that they are part of a larger community consisting of millions of people who ride bikes; instead, they are part of a smaller community consisting of a specific type of cyclist.

Most cyclists typically spend their entire cycling lives functioning within these small units: road riders or mountain bikers or fixie riders or triathletes or cyclocross racers or track racers or people who load their Chihuahua in a basket on a beach cruiser bicycle and ride off in the direction of sunshine and music and groovy people who don't want to sweat life's details.

Each of these groups has its own culture and history and a set of rules and normative behaviors. Let's call these groups Bike Tribes. Each of us is part of one tribal group. Each of us is curious about the other Bike Tribes, too, because in that one special way, because we love having two wheels under us, we're all the same.

THE PEOPLE YOU will meet in this book are part of one Bike Tribe or another, whether they know it or not, and some of them most certainly do not know it. They are not exactly real people, either; they are what is known in the writing trade as *composite characters,* meaning they are fictional people based on a number of real people I have interviewed in the process of preparing this book. I have placed these people in composite situations, too, and have in the process poked more fun at them than their real-life counterparts probably merit. Then again, if it ever comes to pass that cyclists lose the ability to poke fun at themselves and at our sport in general—the odd bikes we ride, the odd clothing, et cetera—the sport of cycling itself will lose its magic.

5

MINDING THE
STORE

From the street, you can see more than 30 road cyclists in garishly bright spandex arranged in various semicircles in the parking lot of *Big Ed's Cyclery* on a Wednesday evening, 5:25 p.m., in late spring.

Some of the riders are skinny to the point of being gaunt and are squatting on their top tubes; some aren't so lean, and they're standing next to their bikes looking apprehensive.

Now Big Ed himself opens the bike shop's glass front door and steps outside. He's tall, 6 foot 4, and he looks happy, especially in the eyes,

---
the Small Shop Owner: ED
---

1. Sandals with socks.

2. Bike-company shirt, obtained free from a sales rep, untucked.

3. Random clutter throughout the shop.

4. Tranquil expression, possibly contemplating a sandwich in the near future.

which are warm and brown and scanning the parking lot and acknowledging all the riders because he knows all of them. Like Tom, the guy who just lost 80 pounds riding his bike. Or Charlotte, who must have lost 50 pounds. Or Bill, the masters state road champion for 4 years running. Ed's customers. His friends. He takes the time to stroll around the lot, greeting everyone and yucking it up, and you would think the guy was the president or something, he's so popular with the riders.

He looks at the sky—overcast but not dark—and the riders keep their eyes fixed on him. He scratches his head finally and announces, "I think we'll go around the lake today!"

Everyone nods or says something on the order of "Right on, man."

Then he steps back in his shop.

He's got about 50K worth of bikes and merchandise in here—a few high-end road bikes and mountain bikes, but most are in the 800-bucks-or-under range because this is a college town. The kids need bikes to get to class a heck of a lot more than they need to show up for the shop's group rides with the local racers. Ed believes that cycling is about people getting from here to there on two wheels, in whatever way suits the individual cyclist best. That's what he tells people, anyway. He's trying to make a living here, and you can't make a living selling $5,000 bikes in a college town.

Still, he loves his Wednesday group ride, which is fast and crazy and sometimes pure-D joy. Sometimes it ends up with people getting grumpy with one another for dropping each other or not waiting up for somebody with a flat tire. You never know what you're going to get, and for the rest of the week, the people who went to the group ride talk about what happened on it. Ed loves that. He loves the college kids. He loves the mountain bikers. He loves the fixie riders and the triathletes and the cruiser riders and, really, anybody who rides and anything having to do with bikes. That's why he's in the business: because he loves it. It sure as hell isn't because he wants to get rich.

Ed's been in the shop since 8 this morning, starting the day by wrenching with George, his mechanic, for 2 hours before opening the shop. Not a bad day at the cash register, either. He sold a cruiser bike and a couple of hybrid bikes and some tires and tubes and whatnot. That's not a great day—after he pays his bills, he's barely breaking even.

Ed pokes his head in the repair area and takes a look at George—55 years old and sturdy and wearing a shop apron and always happy to fiddle with bikes—and says, "How much longer you staying, George?"

George says, "Just finishing this one up. Then I'm out of here."

"Cool," Ed says. "I'm suiting up and rolling with the group. Lock up when you're done, will you?"

George says that he will. Ed didn't need to ask him to lock up, but that's the way Ed is, always finding a way to touch base with people and try to encourage mellowness and happiness in all things. Ed considers himself to be an old bicycle hippie from way back, and he's proud of that.

Ed changes into bike kit and grabs a vintage Steel Colnago—his baby, with down-tube shifters and hand-built wheels—and he rolls it toward the door. He pauses to look around his shop, all the bikes, the wheels, the accessories, the smell of rubber and grease, and he's barely getting by. Every month he covers his financial nut, and that's about it. He works 6 days a week year-round and never takes a vacation. But hey, he loves this life. He wouldn't trade it for anything.

So with this in mind, he opens the door, rolls his bike into the lot, and says to the cyclists gathered there, "Okay, let's go!"

Saturday afternoons are the *worst* at Rock Cycles.

Phil hates everything about them. He's not the owner here. He's the manager, just working for somebody else, some corporation that owns this place, some board of directors who as sure as bikes have wheels are making a mint off his labors. And Saturdays are a horrible circus at best, an insult to his professional injury—to a guy like him who used to love bikes and race bikes and ended up managing a big-box bike shop at the mall.

Look what he has to put up with. This woman at the counter? She disgusts Phil. She looms over him and sneers, with her 10-year-old, future-criminal-looking boy next to her. Phil worries that if he were to extend his index finger over the counter, the woman would bite his finger off and spit it back at him.

She says, "You're the owner. You can give us a better discount than this."

Phil takes one of the many deep breaths he has taken today and says,

---

the Big-Box Shop Manager: PHIL

1. Arms crossed.
2. Shirt tucked in.
3. Irreversible corporate frown on the face.
4. Merchandise displayed in perfect, anal-retentive rows.
5. Brightest possible lights.

"I am the *manager,* not the owner. Four hundred dollars is the best I can do for that bike."

"But I saw that same bike on the Internet for 300."

"True. But we will service the bike for a whole year."

"For free?"

"For free," Phil says. "It's included in the price."

"That's not what I heard. I heard you jack up the prices and promise all sorts of service, then when the bike breaks down, you still charge an arm and a leg for repair."

Phil's eyes drift away from her, past the racks of bikes and clothing and accessories and the wall-size posters of the Tour of California and Lance Armstrong, through the window, and into the parking lot, where Phil sees the woman's shiny new Mercedes-Benz sport-utility vehicle. That car must have cost 80 grand. And she's dickering with him over a hundred bucks?

On other sectors of the shop floor, his classically youthful sales staff of three guys, in matching shirts, is busy dealing with customers. This world, it occurs to Phil, is a hermetically sealed form of medieval bicycle torture.

The woman says, "I think you're arrogant."

Phil says, "I'm sorry, ma'am. But 400 dollars is final. It's a good price and a good service plan." Phil now gazes at the 10-year-old boy and locks eyes with him. "And this guy will really go fast on this bike."

The kid brightens, but the mother darkens.

"Nope," she says. "I'm taking my business to someone more willing to do business with me. Come on, Jayden. We're going to Big Ed's." Phil watches her make a call on her cell phone in the parking lot before she gets in her Benz and drives off.

Damn. What's Phil going to do about people like that? And what's Phil going to do about Big Ed, the old hippie with his hippie bike shop near the university? Big Ed doesn't have to make money on his shop. That's why everybody likes him. Big Ed can ride bikes and be a cool guy and give everybody great deals, and Big Ed's customers will probably nominate him for sainthood, eventually. Phil has only one concern: the bottom line. If Phil can't manage the shop into a profit, the company will find somebody else to do it for him.

He sighs again and wonders how many hundreds of times a day he sighs on this job. Then he wanders into the service area, where his wrenches are working through the backlog.

He stops near the new kid, Steve, a Cat 2 road racer the shop sponsors. Phil asks, "Did you hear that?"

Steve says, "What a pain in the ass."

"That's the problem with the customers," Phil says. "Most of them aren't even cyclists in the first place."

Someday, Phil wants to be a cyclist again, someone who loves bikes and everything associated with them. But for now, the mere thought of a bike is almost too much for him to bear.

The Bike Shop

All Bike Tribes eventually converge in one place:
the bike shop.

That's where the bikes are and where the bike parts are, and if you're lucky, that's where the spirit of any local cycling community lives. It doesn't always happen that the shop has a community spirit, but in the best of circumstances, a local shop is as close as we will ever get to true understanding between the Bike Tribes. The person in charge of the bike shop, therefore, bears an incredible responsibility to the cycling communities the shop serves.

The cyclists expect a lot from this person, too, almost to the point where no individual in the world can possess all the characteristics the cyclists want. To illustrate, here are 20 common attributes cyclists are looking for in an ideal shop owner/manager:

1. Someone who knows everything about bicycles.

2. Somebody who knows the local cyclists by name and also knows what they're like as people off the bike and what they're like as cyclists on the bike.

3. Someone who is friendly and never condescending. Someone who doesn't mind if you look and don't buy.

4. Someone who won't sell you something you don't need.

5. Someone who is an expert mechanic and who knows the right bike for you and the right parts and accessories for you.

6. Someone who will order anything you want and try to match the online retailer's price.

7. Someone who loves to ride.

8. Someone who keeps the shop open late if you need it.

9. Someone who likes all kinds of riders.

10. Someone who is your friend.

11. Someone who isn't in the business to make money.

12. Someone who volunteers the shop's services to the community.

13. Someone who leads the bike community.

14. Someone who will keep his customers on the road.

15. Someone who never gets frustrated or angry.

16. Someone who doesn't care if you hang out in the shop just because you like hanging around in the shop.

17. Someone who loves hearing about your weekend rides.

18. Someone in whom you have total confidence.

19. Someone you can come to, with anything, and not feel ashamed to say what's on your mind.

20. Someone who can heal the sick.

Well, I made up the last couple of items, but they're not far from the truth. Cyclists want a saint to be in charge of a shop—a sort of priest/athlete who has taken a vow of poverty and humility. It's a tough job, long hours dealing with people who aren't always so cheery, and the pay isn't great. Nobody gets rich running a bicycle shop. The profit margin isn't high enough; there aren't enough customers; and in lots of places, winter effectively shuts down the shop for several months a year. This means that to be that person at the helm of a bike shop, you have to be in it for love. In return, the best shop owners and managers are also loved and respected by their cycling communities in ways that few businesspeople are ever loved. In the often-fractious world of cycling, that's no small deal indeed.

THE WRENCH WHO KEEPS
US ROLLING

For Steve, *wrenching* is a means to an end.
If Phil says something—*anything*—Steve has
to agree with whatever he says.

Look at the situation: Phil runs the shop, and the shop sponsors the road-racing team that Steve's on, and what would Steve do if he were cut loose from that team? How could he afford to keep racing bikes at a high level?

So when Phil stops in the repair shop and asks, "You have a good day back here, Steve?" Steve doesn't pause to reflect. He says, "Heck yeah." And he gives Phil a grin the size of first place at the United States Criterium Championships.

---

the Big-Box Shop Mechanic: STEVE

1. The key to the job is the numbers in the computer.
2. Perpetual I-don't-want-to-be-here frown.
3. Perfectly organized work area, both the reason for and the consequence of the frown.

"Excellent," Phil says and returns to the sales floor, which is the best place for a manager to be, in Steve's opinion.

Truth is, Steve's day has been a nightmare twice the length of the nightmare on Elm Street. His legs ache. He's so thirsty he could chug an entire 5-gallon watercooler bottle and still be thirsty, and he's so hungry that he has been considering eating the tube of waterless grease on his work stand. Sure, this is the life of an elite racer—tired, hungry, thirsty—but do elite racers have to spend 10-hour days turning a wrench in a bike shop? He should be spending his recovery time loafing on the couch with his legs elevated and an action-adventure movie on TV.

But no such luck. And there are no races on his schedule today, so here he is, on a Saturday, at work. Because he doesn't have a race this weekend, he has been piling on the miles all week—a couple of hours before work, a couple of hours after work, with intervals, too. He's one hurting unit. Maybe it will pay off. Maybe next year he will be a full-on pro and won't have to suffer the humiliation of this stupid job.

Now Phil returns to the repair area. "Steve, I got a bike for you to look at."

Steve rises dutifully from his stool, his thighs aching beyond belief, and he shuffles toward the service counter. There, with a lower-end aluminum road bike, stands a middle-aged man with graying hair and a button-down shirt tucked into khaki Dockers.

Steve gives the customer the trademark I-care grin and asks, "What's wrong with her?"

The customer points at the right brake-lever hood and says, "Won't shift properly," then he rolls the bike into Steve's grasp.

Steve says, "Nice bike." This is a lie. Steve would rather ride a live elephant than throw his leg over the top tube of this piece of junk. He fingers the shifting mechanism and makes a cursory examination of the bike's drive train and cassette. "How many miles you have on this bike?"

Customer: "Don't know. Had it a few years."

Steve says, "Looks to me like if you put on a new chain and a new cassette—probably new cables, too—she'll shift as good as new."

The customer agrees to this, and Steve lets him know it will be ready in a few days and that's that.

Probably Steve could tweak the limit screws on the bike's derailleur and the bike would shift just fine. But hey, why do a free repair when he can generate at least 200 bucks of repair work for the store?

Middle of the afternoon at Big Ed's Cyclery, George and Big Ed are taking a break by the sales counter.

No customers are in the store, a lull after some hard-core roadies were in the shop around noon wanting tweaks to their bikes before heading out of town to the races. George has a backlog of bikes in the back room—this is summer and the busy season, and he's been working 10-hour days lately, but he's cool with the backlog. He'll get around to it.

George says, "Sure is quiet."

Ed says, "Not for long," then elbows George in the ribs. "Buy you a sandwich?"

George has never once refused a sandwich. He nods to Ed, and Ed heads out the door whistling a happy tune.

Submarine sandwich. George would most certainly click "Like" on a submarine sandwich Facebook page, if there were one, and there probably is one. George would also click "Like" on pizza, TV, NFL football,

---

the Small Shop Mechanic: GEORGE

1. Joyful expression.
2. Shop appears to be a mess, but in fact the mechanic knows exactly where everything is.

Major League Baseball, and the Weather Channel. And Taco Bell, too! Don't forget that!

George, you see, isn't a very complicated person. He knows this and isn't too worried about this. He's hardworking—that's how he would describe himself—and not proud of it, really. He simply is what he is and has no ambition to be more than what he is. He's been working at Big Ed's since it opened 10 years ago, and he's happy here. George has been married to his high school sweetheart—Candace—since he was 18. Thirty-five years of marriage now? Thirty-eight? Candace has been a bank teller since she was 18, and George has been fixing bikes since then. What can he say? When he was a kid, he was good at tinkering with things—lawn mowers, furnaces, you name it—and maybe he could have been an auto mechanic or worked in a small engine shop and made a heck of a lot more money. But something about bikes, about the smell of a bike shop, about the people who come into the shop, made him choose to fix bikes. Here he is, 54 years old, in a bike shop. Not a bad life, really. He looks around at the bikes on the rack. He tweaked each one personally when it came out of the box. He's built wheels for God only knows how many riders. For a moment, he thinks, *Yeah, I'm an artist, all right.* But then the front-door chime rings—a customer's coming in.

The customer is Tom, a schoolteacher in his midthirties who bought his road bike toward the end of last summer and since then has lost probably 80 pounds, could be 100 pounds.

Tom says, "George, I'm sorry, but it's just not shifting right."

George smiles and says he'll take a look and does and can see right away that the rear derailleur is slightly bent on the hangar.

"Take a look-see," George says to Tom and guides him to a position behind the rear wheel, so he can see easily what George is trying to explain. "Derailleur is bent. See how the chainline isn't straight?" George points it out carefully and gives Tom time to comprehend the problem.

Tom says, "Dammit. Will I be able to ride today?"

George says, "I'll show you a magic trick." He grabs the derailleur and bends it by hand back to where it should be. "Pretty cool, no?"

Tom laughs and asks, "Is that it?"

George says, "It'll shift perfect now."

"Thanks, man. How much do I owe you?"

George shakes his head. "Are you kidding me? You don't owe me a cent. Now get out there and ride your bike."

The Mechanics

Because a bicycle is a simple machine—and in terms of the pantheon of machinery throughout history, the bicycle *is* a simple machine—we might assume that the person who repairs bicycles professionally is a simpleminded, *living-in-the-shire* type of soul.

Mechanics can indeed be simple souls, but they can be complicated geniuses, too. They can be people who never ride bikes at all or people who only work in bike shops because they want to buy bikes and parts at cost. They are, like the cyclists who require their services, a varied lot.

One thing is for sure: About the only time cyclists will mention their mechanic is when they feel the mechanic has done a crappy job. That's the nature of cyclists, especially the more serious ones: They are better at complaining than they are at praising. And when things aren't going right on the bike, what better to blame than the bike itself? And who's at fault for problems with the bike? That would be the mechanic. Obviously, it's not *usually* the mechanic's fault, but in the shit-flows-downhill world of cycling, the shop mechanic tends to occupy the lowest portion of the valley floor.

What's worse for the mechanic is that the cyclists are looking for qualities in a mechanic that in fact far exceed the saintlike qualities of the ideal shop owner/manager. We're talking about someone who is timely and accurate and personable and passionate and honest and never makes mistakes and never makes the customer feel stupid and is always happy about everything and really appreciates working for a low hourly wage or, better yet, will do several hours of work on a bicycle in exchange for a $9 six-pack of Belgian beer.

Anything could cross the mechanic's transom. People come in and want their flat tires fixed or they want their chain lubed or they have found a 1978 Schwinn Continental in their garage and want it fixed up and ready to ride by the weekend—or, the worst, a fanatical road racer type will show up on Thursday evening, just before the shop's about to close, and announce that he has a big race on Saturday and needs about 5 hours' worth of work done on the bike before 10:00 a.m. Friday!

The bicycle mechanic really has one behavior option with regard to the person whose bicycle needs fixing: "Yes," the bicycle mechanic must say. "I can do that for you!"

This is not the way it should be, of course. Bike mechanics rarely make much money, and in the summer season, they're sometimes working 10 hours a day, 6 or 7 days a week. What the cyclists should do when they deal with their mechanics is say, "Thanks! I love everything you do!"

BMX

This Thursday night *under the lights,* Randy feels like he's a coiled spring in the starting gate.

That's what his dad told him a few minutes ago. "At that starting line," Randy's dad said, "you gotta be a coiled spring. Then when that gate comes down, you gotta unleash all your energy!" Randy's dad is standing behind the fence next to the track right now, smoking a cigarette and drinking a beer with a cooler sleeve wrapped around it. Randy makes quick eye contact, and his dad nods once. That means it's go time.

Randy presses his front tire into the gate and adjusts his helmet. He puffs out a long breath and gazes forward, down the ramp and over the short straightaway and then into that first banked left-hand

---

the BMX Racer: RANDY

1. Full face helmet.
2. The boy flies through the air with the greatest of ease.
3. Beer.
4. Cigarettes.
5. The crowd watching something other than the race.

turn. That's the tough part, to get there first, to get the hole shot, and Randy by God is going to take that hole shot in this moto if it kills him.

In the first two motos tonight, Terrell, the kid in the gate next to Randy, has been faster down the ramp and more fearless into that first corner. Once Terrell gets ahead, he stays ahead the rest of the race. That's just the deal with Terrell. Kid's good. Randy's good, too. That's what his dad keeps telling him. That's what Terrell keeps telling him, too.

Like now.

Terrell says, "You were fast that last moto."

Randy shakes his head but doesn't say anything.

Randy and Terrell are both 10 years old and both about the same size, and unless Terrell crashes, which almost never happens, Terrell always beats Randy. Randy is always second, which means Randy is faster than the other kids, and that's pretty cool except not nearly as cool as coming in first. The only reason Randy never beats Terrell, according to his dad, is he lets Terrell get into his head.

Terrell says, "But you still ain't gonna beat me."

Randy doesn't answer. His dad says don't talk to Terrell till the race is over. His dad says to pretend Terrell isn't there at the gate.

Terrell asks, "Is your dad racing cruiser division tonight?"

Randy keeps it buttoned up. His dad *will* be racing in the cruiser division—that's the race for dads who used to race BMX when they were kids—and Randy's dad will beat Terrell's dad because Randy's dad always does. Randy thinks about this and decides, for psych-out purposes, to break the maintain-radio-silence-in-the-gate rule.

Randy says, "My dad will totally beat your dad in cruisers."

"Yeah, he will," Terrell says, "but that don't mean you'll ever beat me."

The starter says it's time to get ready. Randy tenses, and for a moment his eyes drift to a light on the pole over the first turn. Moths swarm around the light, and birds fly through and pick them off. It's like a World War II dogfight video game or something. Wow. Must be tough to be a moth going against those birds.

The start light turns green, the gate drops, and it's already too late. Terrell is ahead of Randy before they hit the bottom of the ramp. Randy gives it everything to catch Terrell and beat him to the first turn. His world becomes bumps and hard breathing and jostling shoulders with Terrell and straining every part of his body to push past him. In what he will always remember in slow motion—with clumps of dirt in the air and the bright lights on the poles above the track and a hard-charging sound deep in his heart—Randy breaks first into the corner and gets the hole shot over Terrell. Randy's going to win this moto—no doubt—and he promises himself, while he gives it full gas the rest of the way around the track, that he won't let Terrell get into his head ever again.

BMX

*BMX might be the original cycling melting pot,
the primordial stew where racing-type cyclists
originate.*

When you arrive at a BMX track and hear Ronnie James Dio or Kid Rock blasting from the loudspeakers, you would do well to keep in mind that many celebrated champions in professional cycling have had their beginnings in BMX—the great road racer Robbie McEwen, for instance, or the mountain biker Tinker Juarez. Maybe even you got your start in BMX. Sure enough, BMX requires steel nerves and raw power and excellent handling and the ability to get knocked down in one moto, then get up and win in the next. Think about it: You fly down a ramp and charge full blast to win the hole shot into the first corner, and people are crashing behind you—or they could be crashing in front of you—and that's only the first few seconds of the race!

BMX is tough. It's rough-and-tumble. It also possesses a cultural element missing from most other forms of competitive cycling. At the track, we see proud parents and relatives who are not always in possession of graduate degrees from prestigious universities—and not always the type of folks who follow strict exercise regimens. People smoke cigarettes and drink beer and Mountain Dew with sugar in it. In a word, if there is a true working-class route into the sport of competitive cycling, BMX is that route.

But just because a kid races BMX doesn't mean the Tour de France looms in his future. You have small bikes here, even in the cruiser division, that are basically useless for doing anything other than BMX racing on a curvy, bumpy track. Sure, you occasionally see somebody pedaling a BMX bike hither and yon on the streets of your town, but nobody looks comfortable pedaling a BMX bike to the grocery store. Even though it is now an Olympic sport, BMX doesn't get much respect from, say, century riders or road racers or triathletes. Those are the people who spend their cycling lives on the road and who get squeamish at the mention of the word *dirt* when it appears in close proximity to the word *cycling*. To road riders, comfort and safety are key concepts. On the other hand, any self-respecting mountain biker or cyclocross racer can see people racing BMX and know that it takes amazing skill and strength (in the cruiser division, racers routinely snap crankarms in half), and consequently, mountain bikers and 'crossers think BMX is cool.

THE OVERWHELMING
MAJORITY

On a midmorning in June, William rolls his mountain bike along the bike path.

He stops at a bench alongside the path, leans the bike against a tree, takes a seat, and enjoys the view of trees and the sunlight filtering through the leaves. He is 17 years old, one more year of high school left. He prefers to be called William because he likes the way the name gives the impression that he's a poet. He *is* a poet, too. And he does painting and sculpture. And plays the acoustic guitar. And he's totally into organic, locally grown food and sustainable living.

the High School Cyclists: WILLIAM and KATRIN

1. Old-school bikes. Accept no substitutes.
2. Kick stand, because that's old-school, too.
3. Jeans, because who goes for a bike ride without jeans on?
4. No helmets. High school kids, they just can't help it; they just don't have any common sense.

His girlfriend, Katrin, rolls up on a vintage Schwinn Continental, stops, and sets a foot on the path.

"Ride downtown?" she says and smiles a very pretty smile. She has an elfin look, light-blue eyes, pointy features, ethereal expression. She shares William's love for poetry and for music and for sustainable living and for getting around on bicycles instead of in automobiles.

William rises from the bench and in a dorky British accent says, "With you, my dear, I will ride anywhere."

"Why, William, that is so nice of you to say." She winks.

William thinks she's awesome. She may be a real elf, for all he knows.

They start rolling toward downtown, about 3 miles on the bike path from here. They pedal side by side, in no hurry, and the sunlight dapples the maples along the trail, which William can't help mentioning.

"That sunshine sure does dapple those leaves," he says.

Katrin laughs. "Dapple? Where'd you get that word?"

"Gerard Manley Hopkins."

"Really?"

"'Glory be to God for dappled things.'"

Katrin says, "That certainly is a Manley Hopkins line!"

They laugh for a bit and keep pedaling.

A man in a bright-red spandex suit riding a fancy sort of space-age time trial bike comes toward them on the trail. He is blazing, tilted forward with his hands in his aero bars, eyes invisible behind his sunglasses, and he flies by without acknowledging William and Katrin.

William can feel the wind blowing off the rider when he passes. "Geez, that jerk is sure taking himself seriously," he says.

Katrin smiles and says, "I hope he slows down for that stop sign back there."

"That would suck for him," William says, "if he rode that bike right into traffic."

"Hold up. Maybe he will."

They slow and turn around and look behind them on the trail. No sign of the man in spandex.

William says, "Vanished."

"That's crazy." Katrin pedals down the path again and seems to be thinking about something quite seriously. Finally, she says, "You think Gerard Manley Hopkins would ride a bike like that?"

"That's the ultimate question," William says. "What would Gerard Manley Hopkins do?"

"I'm pretty sure he would *love* that red spandex outfit!"

"Maybe I should get one then?"

"If that helps your poetry," Katrin says, "I'm all for it."

William is just so into riding bikes and hanging out with Katrin that for a second he contemplates buying a skin suit and getting a fancy time trial bike. "You really think that would help?"

"No, you goof," Katrin says. She tells him if he were to buy her a cup of coffee downtown, that would help his poetry a whole lot more. He likes that idea. He believes he will ride just about anywhere to buy Katrin a cup of coffee.

Harriet and Glenda, retired schoolteachers, 62 and 65 years old respectively, don't miss a morning on the bike path *all summer*, except for when the weather's bad, which doesn't happen too often.

Most mornings, they always say to each other, are perfect—cool temperatures, not much wind, not too many people on the path. Every morning at exactly this time, in fact, they put on their SPF 50 and their bike shorts and sleeveless shirts and sensible helmets, and hop on their hybrid bikes. They meet up at the trailhead and roll down the path together and have such a wonderful time.

Harriet says, "Another nice day."

Glenda says, "Yes, it is."

They usually don't chit-chat too much early in their ride, on account

---

the Retiree Cyclists: HARRIET and GLENDA

1. Helmets. After a number of years on this planet, people can't help having common sense.

2. Sensible cycling outfit—purchased online, after much contemplation about color and multiple searches through various Web sites to find the best price.

3. Upright position on the bike.

4. Large bags on the handlebars carrying maps of the bike path, sun block, bug spray, Chapstick, an apple, a banana, a granola bar, and $5 for coffee and a muffin after the ride.

of it takes a while for the bones to get acclimated to pedaling. The path is so nice, trees on both sides and a river alongside it all the way back to downtown. Side-by-side riding. Ideal. They have the whole bike path to themselves.

Harriet coughs and asks, "How many more years you think we can do this?"

Glenda says, "Pfft. A lot more years. How could you even ask that?"

"Oh, I don't want it to end, is all."

"Put that kind of thing right out of your mind, Harriet."

They don't talk for a while—just enjoying each other's company, keeping things positive. The only sound is their tires rolling and chains passing over their sprockets and the sound of summer birds. Glenda feels the ache escaping from her bones and starts pedaling a fraction harder. Harriet matches her, not out of competition but out of a feel for each other's efforts, something they've learned from riding together the last few summers.

Harriet clears her throat again, a habit—it helps to get people's attention before she speaks. At the exact instant she starts to say something, shouts ring out behind them on the trail. Men yelling, "Bikes back!" One man yells, "On your left!" Another yells, "Single file and to the right, please." Sounds like a police officer saying it. "Come on, ladies!"

The ladies immediately quit pedaling and squeeze their bikes close together because they don't know where else to go but toward each other.

One biker passes on their left, a man on a road bicycle wearing a red-and-white spandex racing suit with "Big Ed's Cyclery" on the back.

Then another man dressed just like him passes. Then a third man, in a darker uniform without any writing on it, rolls by and slows and turns his head to the ladies. His sunglasses are so dark his eyes are invisible. He looks almost like a bike-riding robot out of a science-fiction movie. He says, "Remember to stay to the right, ladies. There are other people using this path."

Harriet and Glenda just nod silently, which satisfies the man on the road bike, and he sprints away on the path in pursuit of the other riders he was with. This is all too sudden and too shocking. It feels like three single-engine airplanes have buzzed them suddenly.

The shouting is over, and the three men become a small object evaporating into the horizon of the trail ahead.

The ladies pedal again, slowly. They need to think about this awhile. The sun is out. Not one trace of dew is left on the path-side grass.

Finally, Harriet starts laughing. She says, "Well, it looks like we need to get our shit together. All these years riding the trail—apparently, we haven't been riding it correctly."

Glenda laughs, too. "You know what we need to do? Trade in these bikes for a couple of those fancy bikes. I bet we could teach those young whippersnappers a lesson!"

Harriet says, "*Whippersnappers!* That is *so* funny."

Pretty soon, they're busting a gut laughing. The sting is gone. "Oh, we shouldn't laugh like this," Glenda says. "But did you hear that guy? 'Remember to stay to the right, ladies.' Some people take themselves a little too seriously, let me tell you."

They keep laughing and talking about those guys for the rest of the ride.

The Average Rider

Let's be brutally honest: Most people who ride
bicycles aren't fanatics about cycling.

They are just using bikes to roll from one place to another. They're not
posting pictures of themselves in bicycle gear as the profile picture on
social networking sites, not falling asleep at night with a bicycle catalog
in their hands, not spending a fortune on the clothing they wear to ride
their bicycles. It's important to know this because when we think about
the social stratification of cycling culture—about roadies and mountain
bikers and fixie riders and all the rest of us who make up the Bike
Tribes—we are making distinctions that apply to a mere fraction of the
total cycling population.

So when we (meaning those of us of the more fanatical cycling per-
suasion) behold the cyclist on a hybrid bike, sitting upright, not wearing
Lycra bicycle shorts, not wearing bike shoes or using a clipless pedal
system—a cyclist who doesn't worry about speed or distance or calories
burned or any measurable form of performance—we have to keep in
mind that this is a person who likes to ride, meaning this person is worthy of respect and admiration. We should take joy that one of our fellow
human beings can cruise at an indeterminate pace along a bike path,
with the point of the activity being nothing more than fresh air and
mild exercise and maybe a chance to stop along the way and lean the
bike up against a tree and take a seat on a park bench and reflect on all
that is wonderful on the face of God's green earth. The destination of
this person's ride is rarely somewhere exotic, but indeed the destination

is always noteworthy, for the point of this person's ride is nothing other than the ride itself. And the bicycle's purpose on this earth is for riding, not for the manner in which it is ridden. I think Lao-tzu might have said that, were bicycles around in his time.

In other words, you roadies who think you are hot shit when you're looking down your noses at ladies on a bike path, you need to keep your place in the larger world in perspective. After all, there are a lot more of them than there are of you.

THE OCCASIONALLY
DIRTY

One sunny Saturday morning at the trailhead, Karen and Mary have unloaded their bikes from Mary's Volvo wagon and are getting ready to *mount up* and hit the trail.

It's not the longest trail in the world—about 3 miles each way—but there's a beastly climb near the halfway mark, which is why Karen and Mary come here every Saturday, to do the beastly climb and, of course, enjoy the view once they get to the top. Plus their husbands get to spend some quality time with the children, which is always a fine thing for husbands to do.

Today, they're in for a special treat because the view in the parking lot is

___ the Weekend Mountain Bikers: KAREN and MARY ___

1. Midrange full-suspension bikes, disc brakes, well maintained by the local shop mechanic.

2. Helmets.

3. CamelBaks and bike jerseys.

4. Clipless pedals.

as spectacular as the view will be at the top of the hill. About 20 yards away, near the back of a Hummer 2 with its tailgate open, there is a very tanned, shirtless, muscle-ripped man in spandex shorts stretching on a mat he has placed on the lot's asphalt. The mat is purple. The man is a muscle.

Karen says, "He has amazing flexibility."

Mary chuckles quietly. "You think he's going to stretch all day? Or will we have the pleasure of riding behind him on the trail?"

Karen elbows Mary and says, "You're awful."

The man lies on his back and brings a knee to his chest and holds it there, then switches legs and stretches the other one.

"Wow," Mary says. "I could eat that for breakfast." She winks at Karen and says, "I'm just kidding, maybe, sort of, just a little bit, but not really too much."

"Yeah, right," Karen says and rubs her hands together. "Shall we roll?"

They roll.

The trail is fairly wide—a fire lane in the woods, really—and not too curvy, meaning on the straightaways Karen and Mary can ride safely side by side. It's also not too rocky, meaning they can safely push the pace, which they do. They don't have much breath left to talk to each other.

When they reach the climb, they shift into granny gears and bear down on the pedals to keep a reasonable pace. They can hear each other breathing hard and hear each other's bikes creaking and the small rocks flinging out from under their knobby tires.

Karen says, through heavy breaths, "I really appreciate this time every week." She says this each Saturday and means it.

And Mary always says: "I wouldn't miss this time together for the world."

They lower their heads and keep pedaling toward the top.

Todd *needs* to get this trail ride over with.

He completed his preride stretching and entered the number of minutes it took him to do it, 20, into an ongoing tally of his workouts that he keeps as one long note in his iPhone. Damn, everything takes so much time. He needs to get his butt down that trail and back, and then drive to the gym in time for muscle conditioning class at 11. Then there's indoor rock climbing and lifting and more cardio after that. If he had a choice, he totally would skip this mountain bike nonsense and stay at the gym, but his personal trainer—the lovely triathlete Chareesa from the gym—told him he needs to keep his workouts fresh and varied. This means every 10 days or so, like it or not, he goes mountain biking.

Without much enthusiasm, he pulls on an Under Armour sleeveless shirt, puts on his helmet, and jumps on his bike. He doesn't even take one easy pedal stroke before laying the wood to the pedals, gritting his teeth, getting up to speed as quickly as possible, and then holding it. In a finger snap, he's sailing along the trail full tilt, breathing hard and tearing his heart inside out. He remembers seeing those two women take off on the trail before him, and he decides this will give him a reason to push hard: He's going to catch and pass those women before they get to the hill.

He gets serious. He grinds. He pushes down and rocks the bike and gasps for air and feels almost dizzy hurtling down the trail. He keeps going and keeps going and keeps going. He should be passing those women soon. But now he's on the hill, and it's getting really steep, and

he's grinding it as hard as he can upward. The women must have turned off somewhere.

When he finally reaches the top, the two women are standing near their bikes, talking with each other and watching him on his bike.

One of the women says, "Wow, you were really going for it!"

Todd doesn't know what to say. He's breathing too hard to form a word. So he nods and tries to say, "Yeah," then he looks at his watch, takes a deep breath, and heads down the hill. He doesn't like descending as much as he likes climbing because if he falls and scrapes himself, (1) he won't be able to finish the rest of the day's workouts, and (2) he will look horrible at the club tonight, and if he looks horrible, his chances with the ladies will be exactly zero. So to keep safe on the way down, he keeps his hands on the brakes, perches himself with his butt back over the saddle, and tightens his abs to hold his balance.

Suddenly, he hears a woman's voice behind him. "On your left," it says.

Two pastel blurs speed past him down the hill.

The second blur says, "Hi! Nice day for riding, don't you think?"

The women disappear ahead of him, and there's nothing Todd can do about it.

<hr />

the Weekend Mountain Biker: TODD

1. Maximum intensity.

2. Wobbly track left on the trail: Proof that sometimes maximum intensity doesn't translate to maximum speed.

The Casual Mountain Biker

When you first see the casual mountain bike rider, you *will not* see this person riding.

You will see this person driving a car, with a bicycle on a roof or rear rack, heading presumably to a trailhead and then to an exhilarating period of dirt and logs and gnarly drop-offs and such. Well, probably not the gnarly drop-offs, or at least we hope that the casual mountain biker has the good horse sense to play it safe on the trails. One thing is certain: Casual mountain bikers don't necessarily list cycling as their top sport, which is to say they often possess a multidisciplinary athletic background and mind-set and consequently maintain a training regimen that is as varied as their mind-set. The casual mountain biker, therefore, is often a person who may assign one day of the week for mountain biking as a way to maintain a varied, healthy lifestyle.

A COMMON EXERCISE schedule for this type of rider may look like this:

MONDAY: Boot Camp class
TUESDAY: Spinning and muscle conditioning class
WEDNESDAY: Cardio kickboxing
THURSDAY: Running; indoor rock climbing
FRIDAY: Boot Camp class
SATURDAY: Mountain biking
SUNDAY: Golf? TV? Go to the movies?

Maybe the schedule isn't this tight, or maybe it's tighter, but what we find in the casual mountain biker is a person desiring to keep the routine fresh and varied. And what better way to do this than to hit the trails Saturday morning and enjoy some fresh air and clean smells and add some adrenaline to the mix, too!

The casual mountain biker is rarely seen alone—not at the gym, not on the trails. This desire to be with other human beings is something that never should be denigrated because, at its core, cycling is always better when done in groups than in solitude.

In practical terms, the casual mountain biker's engagement with cycling makes a lot of sense because (1) there is more to life than cycling and (2) there are few dumber things to do in this world than going mountain biking alone on technical trails with minimal skills. The wise mountain biker always brings someone along to help pick up the pieces. In moral terms, the casual mountain biker scores points for endeavoring to make the cycling experience a group experience.

From these ranks, few go on to become fanatic cyclists—people whose every breath somehow amplifies a life on two wheels—and few spend vast amounts of money on their equipment. But when they are driving to the trail, people in the community can see bikes on top of cars, and in this sense they are unwitting ambassadors for the sport of cycling. So when on weekends you see these folks on the not-too-technical trails in their baggy shorts and T-shirts and helmets with visors and CamelBaks, you should take heart and say hello. They will most definitely be happy to see you.

THE SHRINKING
PEOPLE

Charlotte has a lot of explaining to do.
She knows this.

She started going to Spinning class at the gym on New Year's Day, and after that went to Spinning class 6 days a week, sometimes 7, and sometimes to two Spinning classes a day. She cut cheese out of her diet (along with the rest of the fatty, fast-food trash she had been eating for so many years) and made a habit of recording her daily calories in a journal and closely monitoring the ratio between the calories she took in and the calories she expended. It worked. She began to shrink, little by little, then a lot by a lot.

Spinning was the key to this. She loved Spinning, and by extension, she thought she might love cycling? So when the weather warmed up, she spent $2,500 on a carbon fiber women's-specific road bike, which she

the Weight-Loss Cyclist: CHARLOTTE

1. This is fun but brutally hard.

2. This isn't so brutally hard anymore.

3. Wow, this is easy.

4. This is fun but brutally hard—and brutally *fast,* too.

has since been riding before work, after work, and all day both days every weekend, rain or shine. Six months into this, she's lost a lot of weight, like at least a couple of tons of weight. People think she's lost her mind. People think she's dying. She is certainly not dying, is what she will tell you. She is finally coming to life! She is a new person: more confident, quick-witted, and definitely brighter in every way. In fact, some people don't even recognize her when they see her out and about in town. If that doesn't mean she's a new person, what does?

So today, after a nifty 35-mile ride, she stops at the coffee shop, still in her sweaty bike clothes, and buys a skim milk latte—no sugar, 75 calories—and takes it outside to drink in the sun. Nice day. Nice table. She smiles at everyone with a confidence she can never remember having, and the people smile back. She jots down her 75 calories in a little spiral notebook she carries in a baggie in the back pocket of her jersey—pages and pages of what she's eaten on bike rides: energy bars, Gatorade, gels, the occasional turkey sandwich, and so on. What a great system this is for losing weight. She's proud of the way she's been sticking to it.

She looks up from her notebook, and there stands her old friend Melody from high school. Or maybe old *acquaintance* is a better term. Melody was a popular girl in high school, skinny, on the cheerleading squad, on homecoming court. Charlotte was unnoticed and in the shadows.

Melody asks, without bothering to say hello, "What's going on with *you*?"

Charlotte knows the drill. People have been asking her the same thing everywhere she goes. "I've been riding my bike," she says and points to it, pink handlebar tape and all.

"Are you okay?" Melody asks. "You're not *ill* or something, are you?"

Charlotte shakes her head no and asks the question to which she already knows the answer: "Why do you ask?"

"You've lost so much weight!"

Charlotte allows Melody's comment to float in the void between them and takes a deep, practiced breath. "Yep," she says. "I've lost 75 tons so far."

Melody frowns in a quizzical way, and in this pause, Charlotte observes with some satisfaction that Melody—once the object of all the boys' affections—now looks positively dumpy these days. Twenty years later, Charlotte thinks, and life has a way of leveling out.

Melody asks, "And you lost this on purpose?"

"Yes, ma'am."

"Oh," Melody says, almost as if she's disappointed, like it would have been better if Charlotte had said she was dying of a rare disease that causes people to shrink near the end of their lives and wear bicycle clothing and keep journals of the food they eat every day.

Finally, Melody says, "Good for you, Charlotte." Then she walks to the parking lot and gets into a minivan, looking like she's having trouble stuffing herself into the driver's seat before she turns the ignition and drives away.

Charlotte takes a reflective sip of her latte and feels an amazing joyful glow spreading through her body. She is really doing this. She is so much smaller than she used to be. Even her gestures are so much more lithe, so much quicker than they used to be. She never could have lost all this weight on a treadmill. No way. Treadmills are a drag. But cycling is totally fun! She is going to do this for the rest of her life, no doubt about it, and her life is going to be amazingly happy.

She finishes her latte and with huge satisfaction gets back on her bike and begins her ride home. How much you want to bet she'll take the long way?

Tom believes it's bad luck to talk about the miracle that has occurred. Last year, he was what you call "280 pounds of heavenly joy" struggling to pedal a bicycle down a flat road, let alone try to lug his guts up even the slightest incline. But look at him now: 175 pounds with clothes on, rolling his bike out of Big Ed's Cyclery after getting it fixed for free. Only the fastest cyclists in town get that kind of treatment at the bike shop. And you know what this means? Tom is a real rider now.

He leans his bike against his Volvo in the parking lot and can see his reflection in the shop window. Short hair. Trim waist. T-shirt tucked into his jeans. Is that person really him? Long ago, he used to like the expression "If you met yourself on the street, you wouldn't know yourself." He used to think of that as a metaphor, as something that represented a larger truth about self-awareness, but now? He honestly doesn't know himself when he sees himself. That's awesome, no? He used to be what people would call "a jolly fat guy." Now he's a jolly *fast* guy.

the Weight-Loss Cyclist: TOM

1. Jeans are 33 inches at the waist and hanging loose
2. Large T-shirt (should be a medium)
3. Man, is that really who I used to be?
4. Jeans are 44 inches at the waist and fit snugly.
5. Man, is that who I can become if I ride bikes?

A Kia with a bike rack on the roof pulls into the lot, and out pops Bill, whom everybody on group ride affectionately calls The Beast, because Bill is the strongest rider in town—a guy who's won the state championships a bunch of times. Bill's in his forties, lean, not too tall, and has hard gray eyes that he fixes on Tom.

"Hey, Tom," Bill says. "Fun times on group ride this week, no?"

Group ride was crazy on Wednesday. Some people from out of town showed up and attacked off the front and ended up getting lost, because they didn't know what route the group was taking.

Tom laughs and says the only stupid word that comes to his head. "Awesome."

"Bunch of jackasses on group ride," Bill says and laughs. "You riding today?"

Tom nods in the affirmative.

Bill says, "I'm rolling in about an hour. Wanna come along?"

Tom feels as if a shaft of light has focused on him on a dark stage, like at last he has been chosen to join the great ones on the local hallowed roads of cycling. He can almost hear music in the background of this moment, a joyful orchestra announcing that the day to matriculate into the ranks of the truly fast cyclists has finally come. Tom says, "Hell yeah."

"Meet you here in an hour," Bill says and heads inside the shop.

The Weight-Loss Cyclist

Of all the true fanatics, zealots, and believers in a life lived on two wheels, the person who has lost significant weight because of cycling resides at the top of the list.

Cycling, you see, is a nearly perfect form of exercise to promote weight loss. For one thing, it's at least 7,000 times more fun than, say, chugging along on a StairMaster. For another, if a person cycles moderately for an hour or two a day over the course of a summer—pedaling with a high, easy-spinning cadence (this keeps the heart rate lower and burns fat)—and if during this period a person makes sure to ease back on the double-cheese pizzas, the weight will disappear as if it's an anvil falling off a cliff into the sea.

When this happens, when the weight comes off, there is no greater joy on this earth. It's even better than being in love! Not only has this person lost weight, but in the process, invariably, this person has gotten incredibly faster on a bike. If a person can apply the same power to the pedals with 40 or 50 or 60 or even 100 fewer pounds on the bike—wow, look out! This word may be overused, but I'm going to use it anyway, because it's the most precise possible word to apply to a person who successfully lost weight through cycling: woohoo!

Can I say it again, just because it's so true?

Woohoo!

Thank you.

And that's exactly why weight-loss cyclists are so fanatical about cycling. They know the sport has helped them lose weight and, in the process of losing weight, they have acquired a newer, skinnier identity, and what else would that identity be but fanatical cyclist!

There is a price to losing weight through cycling, of course, but it's a price most weight-loss cyclists are happy to pay. Or maybe it's an ironic price. For the overweight cyclist—and we're talking in the range of 50 to 100 pounds overweight—there are extremely limited options with respect to clothing and equipment. This is because cycling, in its elite form, is a sport for extremely skinny people, people who are bones with leg muscles attached to them, people who look sort of like an upside-down chicken drumstick. And the way equipment is sold to regular people who ride bikes seriously is by association with the skinniest, freakiest, fastest people in the sport—we're talking about 145-pound men who race in the Giro d'Italia. If a 300-pound person even sits on some of this stuff, it will crumble beneath them. Same is true for the clothing. Jerseys and bike shorts and undershirts, the very same items of clothing that make cycling more comfortable for professional riders, are not available for heavier riders.

So if you're way overweight, you apparently don't get to ride comfortably till you've lost the weight. This is a sad variation on the old adage "You can't get a job till you already have a job." And honestly, it sucks. Heavy cyclists often have to ride on rear wheels designed for tandems and wear XXX T-shirts that feel like they're made out of World War II tent canvas. Nevertheless, those who persevere through the weight-loss period are rewarded when they find themselves able to buy the nice equipment designed for skinny people. This may cost thousands of dollars—new bike, new wheels, all new clothing, et cetera—but you will never see a happier human being than someone who has lost a bunch of weight and gets to buy a whole lot of new stuff.

ONE PART OF
THREE PARTS

Tuesday evening, Brett experiences some confusion.

He finished swimming 72 lengths of the gym's pool and toweled off and pulled on his bike shorts and jogged to his car and removed his bike from the roof rack and changed quickly into his cycling shoes and—bam!—he's on his bike and on the road, immediately hunkered over his aero bars and holding his speed steady at 17.1 miles per hour toward the countryside. He's going to ride a circuit of 21.2 miles and then do a 5-mile run, and after that he should be about ready to go to bed.

He's pedaling evenly, he guesses, and is making sure not to drop below 17 miles per hour, which should mean things are peaches and

---
the Slow Triathlete: BRETT

1. Abrasions on right knee from numerous parking-lot crashes that occurred while practicing transitions.
2. Eternal grimace: This is not fun; this is work.
3. Handlebar-mounted water bottle, with straw.

---

cream. But something's eating at him: Did he really swim 72 lengths? Maybe he lost count somewhere and either jumped ahead by a couple of lengths or, worse, did only 70 lengths or maybe even only 68, which would mean he's not doing the full workout by four full lengths of the pool! Will this mean when he does the triathlon on Saturday it will be a disaster?

Dammit. How could he have spaced that out? He keeps running the lap numbers and the calamitous permutations of the lap numbers and is starting to become angry with himself and suddenly, his speed has dropped to 16.2 miles per hour. What an inexcusable lapse of concentration! He pushes a little harder and gets the speed back up to 17.2 and takes a sip from the straw that's attached to his water bottle that's attached to his bike. No hands, of course. He needs to stay in his aero bars at all times because the slightest lift of the head, the slightest instant when he is not stretched over those bars, will cost him seconds and more likely minutes during the actual tri.

70. 72. 74. 68. 66. He can't get his mind off it. He may be going crazy.

Up ahead, there's a stop sign and traffic on the cross street, meaning he'll have to roll to a stop and his average speed for the bike workout will be shot to hell. Is anything going to go right this evening? He stops and fumes and waits for a couple of cars to pass, then he's pedaling again, in the aero bars, and thinking maybe if he can hold 19 miles per hour for a while he'll be back up to the proper average speed. He strains and breathes hard and grips the bars with all his might, but he can barely hold 19 miles per hour. His speed is 17, always is, and if he can't hold that, he might as well stay home and watch TV.

But he might be in luck. He sees three people on bikes a ways up the road, and this gives him motivation to keep pushing hard till he can catch them and pass them. Doesn't take long, either—seems like he's pulling up on them in no time flat. The riders are three skinny guys in matching Big Ed's Cyclery uniforms, riding three abreast and apparently talking with each other with considerable emotion, riding their bikes with one hand and gesticulating with the other. Brett keeps his effort dialed in and whizzes by them and feels really strong about it because, if you think about it, shouldn't bike racers be riding a whole lot faster than those guys?

He hears this behind him: "Jackass." But he's not sure that's the word. Then he hears a whistling noise, and one-two-three the Big Ed's racers fly past him. The third one in line says, "Don't take yourself so seriously. You're slow." In seconds they are at least a hundred yards up the road and looking smaller and smaller, in exact proportion to the way Brett's self-confidence on the bike is feeling smaller and smaller.

Those guys, Brett thinks, are assholes.

Sarah keeps one word in her head: *Saturday.*

That's her big day, the culmination of her exercise goal for the last 10 weeks, which has been to compete in her first triathlon. She knows the tri is going to be really tough and that she is going to have to ask effort of herself that she's never asked before. But she's hoping the triathlon experience will be fun, too, because that's what exercise is supposed to be about: fun!

At the moment, after work on Tuesday evening, she's not exactly having the most fun she's ever had in her life. She's riding her hybrid on the bike path outside of town, and the headwind is so horrible she can hardly pedal into it. One more gust and she might tip over. What if there's a wind like this on Saturday? Oh my gosh, she may not finish. Wouldn't that be embarrassing?

Here's a bench along the trail, perfectly placed and coming at exactly the correct time to allow Sarah to get her positive attitude back. She decides to take a break and call Chareesa, her trainer, and ask for help.

the Beginner Triathlete: SARAH

1. Look of confusion and/or terror.
2. Pedals with toe clips.
3. Unused aero bars, because it's just too darn hard to ride a bike holding on to aero bars.

Sarah takes a seat on the bench. Thirty-four years old and calling her trainer like she would call her mom! The wind howls over the path and shakes the leaves and bends the trees. Sarah dials and shields her cell phone from the wind.

When Chareesa answers in her rough, gravelly voice, Sarah immediately feels ashamed about calling.

"Chareesa," Sarah says, "I think I'm going to cry."

"What's the matter?" Chareesa asks. She has a jock's voice. A voice that yells at people a lot.

Sarah says, "It's really windy and I'm having a hard time riding my bike out here, and, gosh, I'm just so nervous about Saturday."

"Sarah, are you listening to me?"

"Yes."

"You'll do fine on Saturday. It's your first triathlon. You don't have to set the course on fire."

"But what if I can't finish?"

"Sarah, what did you just say?"

Sarah gazes up and down the path. The wind whips the leaves. Dirt blows over the path. But the sun is out. This is a nice enough day, really. So she says, "I'm just nervous about Saturday, I guess."

"Listen to me," Chareesa says. "You're doing great. And you *will* finish. Then we'll start training for the next one and for the next one after that."

"And the next one after that," Sarah says.

"That's my girl," Chareesa says. "Now get back out there and kick your workout in the butt."

Sarah puts the phone away and takes a long, refreshing breath of wind, and she does the right thing. She gets back on her bike. It's not going to be easy, no doubt about that, and maybe it will never be easy, but sooner or later, maybe it won't be so hard.

Chareesa sometimes tires of nurturing people, of bucking them up when they're down, of making them feel they're strong enough to achieve what they wouldn't *otherwise* achieve.

True enough, that's the unavoidable nature of the personal-training trade. She has to be encouraging and friendly and able to design exercise programs to meet the clients' needs and also to make sure that the clients stay on their programs—because that's where the money is, with people who stay on their programs—but once in a while she wishes she could tell people to leave her alone so she can do her own training. She's on a regimen, too. Do any of her clients care about that? It's all about *them*.

Maybe it's not as bad as all that. She's off her bike now and having a mellow moment in the gym's parking lot after riding 15.6 miles at an average of 21.3 miles per hour, which is damn good considering the wind today. Chareesa tries to be honest with herself concerning her performance on the bike. Of all the aspects of triathlon, the bike is the part she dislikes the most. It's uncomfortable. It's expensive. It's unnatural. Not to mention she's just not a biker and will never be a biker. So for her—she's laying it out there honestly—the bike is a total drag. The only reason she

rides as hard as she does is so she can get off the bike and get away from the bike as soon as possible and get back to doing something she enjoys, which is essentially any form of exercise other than riding a triathlon bike. Hell, she doesn't even like to teach indoor cycling! Why would she want to ride a bike in a competitive environment like a triathlon?

She knows the answer: because she's good at it. But that's not too much comfort.

She stuffs her bike in her minivan and takes out a little notebook to record her training. She could easily use her computer to write this stuff down—that's what she asks her own clients to do—but Erik, *her* trainer, insists that she do everything old school, writing her numbers down by hand, charting progress on paper, paper being a substance (he's fond of saying) that you can spread out on a table and analyze. She wants to tell him that's what she hates, to sit and analyze things for hours on end. She wants to stay moving. Moving makes her happy. Sitting makes her fat. Fat makes her unhappy. But Erik would call her a whiner for talking like that.

Now she hears her name and sees Jill, one of the other instructors at the gym, trotting across the parking lot. Jill is essentially the same person as Chareesa: active, driven, hyper, easily bored. They both work out all day, 7 days a week, and when they're not working out, they're finding ways to relax in an active way: dancing, hiking, playing volleyball, kayaking, et cetera.

_____ the Fast Female Triathlete: CHAREESA _____

1. Relaxed, almost disinterested facial expression.
2. A body so fit that it makes other fit people think they're out of shape.
3. Really expensive bicycle and wheels, also the only bike she owns.

Jill asks, "How was the ride?"

Chareesa says, "Necessary."

"I hear that," Jill says. "But the bike's key to the tri."

"The bike's key to my misery, I'm telling you."

Jill says, "What are we gonna do? The clients want to do tri, so we have to do tri."

"It sucks leading by example sometimes," Chareesa says.

"You're so crazy," Jill says and pats Chareesa's shoulder. "So you wanna go for a run? That'll cheer you up."

Chareesa glances at her running shoes in the back of her minivan. "Are you kidding me? I am *dying* to go for a run."

The bald man *under the lights* and in front of the camera is Erik.

He's super fit, monstrously fit, brutally fit, fitter than he has ever been in his 48 years on this earth, fit-like-a-wild-beast fit, fit-like-his-life-

the Guru Triathlete: ERIK

1. Numerous stories that prove that if you train like him, you can be as great as he is.

2. Confident expression; makes you want to pay him for advice.

3. The Ironman logo. He's got it tattooed several places on his body. If you'd like to see them, just ask.

70

is-perfectly-balanced fit. And considering that he was once a collegiate swimmer who almost made it on the Olympic team in the 400 individual medley, his current level of fitness says a whole lot about just how amazingly fit he is. He knows about sacrifice and struggle and hard work and *intelligent* work. He has completed the Ironman distance 37 times, including 10 straight years at the real Ironman in Hawaii. He has raced Olympic-distance triathlons and duathlons and has competed in masters swim meets more times than he could ever remember.

"Look at me," he says into the camera, with a huge, confident grin. "I'm 48 years old and not only look great but feel great. With my training system, you will, too!"

He stares into the camera and gives a thumbs-up and maintains an exaggerated smile till finally he feels the strain of the smile. He shifts his eyes to the bored, sloppy-looking kid operating the camera. "That good enough?" Erik asks.

The kid, who is 23 and chubby and a TV-production whiz at the community college, says, "Looks great. You did awesome."

Erik says, "All right then." He rises from the table and runs his hand over his chin and keeps his eyes on the kid.

The kid is soft and pasty, with dark circles under his eyes—probably only goes outside at night, if at all.

"You're a businessman, right?" Erik asks.

The kid says, "I guess."

"That means you have good business sense, right?"

The kid stares at Erik and doesn't say anything.

Erik says, "So everybody says you're the best video guy in town."

Erik lards it on a bit more, talks about the kid's magnificent reputation and how he's so honored to have the kid working on the project and how he's sure the final product, this kick-ass promotional video, will be the deal maker for his coaching business and how when this thing hits the Internet, Erik will have so many clients that he'll have to hire a number of coaches and probably buy a corporate building and maybe even set up offices in New York and Los Angeles.

"We're talking about a vast international business," Erik says, "and you will have been part of it from the ground floor up."

The kid's face doesn't even twitch.

Erik says, "So what about *this*? I can offer you, free of charge, 2 full years of coaching, the deluxe package, with the 24-hour e-mail and text-message help line, and I guarantee you, within weeks, you'll feel better, you'll lose weight, you'll be more popular with the ladies, and hey, what's not to like about all that?"

The kid: implacable.

Erik says, "So in trade for that, you can comp me the video production costs. You'll be coming out, value-wise, at least $3,000 ahead! Now, I don't know about you, but that's what I call a bargain."

The kid's head finally moves. "Twelve hundred for the video," the kid says and shrugs and starts taking the camera off the tripod. "That's it."

For the first time in a long, long time, Erik honestly doesn't know what to say. Could the kid with the camera be that stupid?

The Triathlete

Triathletes are *made,* not *born.*

Nobody emerges from the womb with an express desire to swim over open water in a large pack of other swimmers and get kicked in the head and elbowed in the ribs, only to emerge from the water and then ride a time trial bike for up to 112 miles in a swimsuit! And then, in the case of Ironman races, run up to a full marathon! It's crazy. It's insanity. It's foolishness. But still, according to triathletes, tri is one of the greatest experiences a person can have.

Maybe they're right. True enough, if you consider what kind of commitment it takes to train for and complete a full Ironman distance—2.4-mile swim, 112-mile bike, 26.219-mile run—you can't help admiring the guts and determination and moxie it takes to do it. You have to tip your hat. Within the group of tri people themselves, in fact, there is much tipping of hats. More than any other sport involving cycling, the triathlon community supports its own and is incredibly encouraging to even the slowest, most meager members of the community. They all tip their hats to each other, in other words, and it's wonderful to see.

However, the bicycle is a means to an end for the triathlete. The bicycle is one part of three parts, not an activity unto itself, and other cyclists—roadies in particular—regard triathletes with rather pointed disdain, a disdain that is never lost on triathletes when they come into contact with roadies. The reason for this disdain is quite simple, really, starting with the tri bike itself—a time trial bike—designed obviously not to be ridden in groups but ridden alone; and, in fact, if you draft off another rider in a tri, you will be penalized (that's in a race, not on a random Tuesday night). What happens, then, is triathletes tend to train all the time in a manner that simulates race conditions—alone, with their hands on the aero bars, trying to maintain a steady-eddie speed. Not surprisingly, because of the highly individual nature of people in tri and because they ride bikes at all times as if they were riding in an official event, tri people often have a tough time interacting with roadies, whose very nature is to be interactive, to ride in groups and speed up and slow down and draft and attack. If a triathlete shows up at a local group road ride, the tri person will invariably receive earful after earful from the roadies, especially when the tri person is trying to ride in the pack with hands on the aero bars (which is dangerous, we must admit).

So what's a tri person to do? Most roadies will say that all the problems will be solved if the tri people just spend more time riding a regular road bike and not pretending all of life is a race. Most Ironman triathletes will say, hey, the only way to prepare the body for an event of that magnitude is to train at the steady rate the event requires.

Whosoever solves this conflict will hold the key to world peace.

RIDERS OF THE
CENTURY

Fifty-five miles into the *Orchard Century*, not far past the aid station—where he didn't stop to pee and fill his bottles with fresh sports drink because he just couldn't afford to lose the time—Ken wonders who the unknown rider is up the road.

The unknown rider has been up there for 20 miles, a few hundred yards in front of Ken, in a red jersey, a hazy form pedaling along the road, and Ken just can't seem to contact him. When Ken pushes to get closer, it seems as if the rider senses Ken's approach and then pushes harder, too. Ken is beginning to think either the guy has ESP or he's wearing a helmet mirror.

Not to worry, though. There are 45 miles left in the century, and in

the Strong Century Rider: KEN

1. Relaxed position on the bike, hands on the tops, grinding it out.
2. Mustache, because *Magnum, P.I.* has never gone out of style.

Ken's experience, unknown riders up the road almost never stay up the road. Ken will catch that rider eventually, because all unknown riders wear down sooner or later.

The day is perfect for a century ride. Seventy degrees. Cloudy. No wind to speak of. Ken's legs feel great, even though this is the 14th organized century he's done in 8 weeks. Usually he does one on Saturday and one on Sunday. This is a Saturday century, and he has one coming up tomorrow and should probably be taking it easy during this one, but he figures if he's got the gas in the tank, he might as well use it. He will eat like a horse tonight and again tomorrow morning and won't have any problems with the next century. That's why he rides all these centuries in the first place—so he can eat as much as he wants. And make no misinterpretation of the facts of Ken: He wants to eat it all.

So the unknown rider up the road? Ken's going to catch him, or at least he's not going to call off the chase till the bitter end, but Ken doubts it will take that long. Besides, there's somebody behind Ken, too, somebody who thinks Ken's an unknown rider and is surging to catch Ken with the same confidence that Ken has been surging to catch the rider in front of him. Ken is so sure somebody's trying to chase him down that he doesn't bother looking backward. At this point in every century—just past halfway—the riders are strung out to hell and gone and are chasing or being chased. Ken isn't sure why this happens, but for Ken, between mile 50 and mile 80 or so, the strategy is to pull himself together and push himself forward, not stressing about how other people are feeling but only concentrating on how he is feeling.

For the time being, he's together. He's pedaling well. He's mostly happy. He's 45 years old and loving the cycling lifestyle, which for him means centuries on the weekends and 50-mile rides every morning before work, except Friday, which is his day off the bike. That's a lot of miles and a lot of time alone riding a bike. Once in a while at this point in a century, when the unknown riders are up and back for miles each way, he wonders what would happen if the unknown riders in his vicinity were to slow down or speed up till they joined together in a group, not necessarily a huge group but a group of maybe five or 10 riders. Would they laugh and talk about bikes and long training rides? Would they introduce themselves and tell stories? One time, Ken thinks. Just one time he would like to see that happen. Because sometimes he gets to feeling lonely out here.

Fred and Ellen have reached the *55-mile aid station* in the Orchard Century and leaned their bikes against a nifty shade tree.

Now they are examining the goodies available for the participants: a long table piled with homemade cookies and fresh fruit and peanut butter sandwiches, along with a 5-gallon container of sports drink and another container the same size full of water.

"And what's this?" Fred asks. "Coffee?"

Ellen laughs because, sure enough, on the ground behind the table she sees a Thermos with a strip of masking tape that has "COFFEE" written on it.

Behind the table stands a pleasantly plump lady in her fifties who seems to be handling her aid-station duties as if she were placed in charge of a goodie table on the planet Jupiter.

The lady says, "The coffee is for the volunteers."

Fred winks at the lady and says, "My wife and I are volunteers."

---

the Good-Time Century Riders: FRED and ELLEN

1. Food in hand, food in bag–why ride 100 miles if you can't eat as much as you want?

2. Happy faces, because this is supposed to be fun, not a day of suffering.

3. Cycling sandals with socks, because comfort is key, and mellow is as mellow does.

Ellen says, "Yeah, we volunteer to drink coffee wherever we go. *And* we have relatives in Tennessee."

Fred says, "Tennessee Volunteers. Get it?"

The lady appears not sure whether to laugh or be angry or come out and say what's probably on her mind: Why on earth do you people want to ride 100 miles in the first place?

On the road, riders roll by individually or in occasional groups of two or three. A few of these riders roll into the aid station and set their bikes down and make their way to the chemical toilets or over to the 5-gallon containers to refill bottles.

Ellen asks, "Please? Two little cups of coffee? They can be small."

The lady finally smiles and says, "I suppose it won't hurt anything."

A minute or so later, Fred and Ellen are leaning against the shade tree next to their bikes, with coffee and brownies and their shoulders pressing together.

Fred asks, "You having a nice time?" Ellen says, "The best. What a beautiful day!"

An old man—maybe in his seventies—pedals by with his head down and with his body rocking. The old man's got the proverbial bit between his teeth.

Fred says, "See that guy? That's who I want to be when I grow up."

Ellen says, "Good luck with that."

"Looks like that old fart's going to beat us soundly to the finish today."

Ellen takes a reflective sip of coffee and says, "Good for him."

"That's right," Fred says. "Good for him."

They lean into each other, and anyone who might see them would immediately know the truth: They are really happy.

Mark is going to *make it.*

All 100 miles of the Orchard Century. In the bag. Wrapped up. And ain't nobody can ever take it away from him that he rode his bicycle 100 miles in 1 day.

He can see the finish line now—can't be half a mile away, maybe closer than that—and he tries picking up his speed but can't muster it. His body's cooked in every imaginable way. His lower back hurts, his neck hurts, his stomach's sour, his calves have been cramping for the last 50 miles, and honestly, he's been wanting to quit since mile 15! He holds up his head as best he can and aims for the line and tries not to let anybody know how much he's hurting.

And what a festive line it is! There's an inflatable arch stretched over the road and a couple of party tents set up in a huge parking lot past the line. He can hear rock music blaring and can smell barbecue, and everything on the road begins to take on more meaning, as if he's ridden through this 100-mile crucible of misery only to arrive at a sort of joyful county fair that has been set up personally for him!

When he rolls over the line, some high school cheerleaders are clapping and pumping fists in the air.

"Good job," the cheerleaders say. "Way to go!"

"Thanks!" he says and begins to well up with tears. He's been riding 10 hours a week for 2 months getting ready for this day, and he sure

enough took a pounding out there, but all that's in the rearview mirror now. He made it.

He rolls to a stop and with much pain gets off his bike and looks at his cyclecomputer: 100.4 miles. A little extra distance, *and* his elapsed time is 6 hours and 32 minutes, almost half an hour better than even his grandest dream time.

He hears his name now and turns to the voice: Maria, his fiancée. She hugs him and says, "You made it! I'm so proud of you."

Mark grins at her so hugely that his cheeks hurt. He loves her so much, which he tells her and hugs her and weeps with joy.

"Are you okay, Mark?"

"Hell yeah," Mark says. He holds up his head and wipes his eyes and scans the busy scene in the finish area, the riders, the families, the band playing in the tent. "Next time, I'm going to do this in under 6 hours."

the First-Time Century Finisher: MARK

1. Fist pump. For the rest of his life, he will remember this moment.

The Century Rider

Ah, the axle around which our sport revolves, the bottom bracket around which our crank turns, the grease in our cable housings, the carbon fiber in our down tube, that most essential cyclist to the sport of cycling, that person you see with the Trek Madone and the yellow/gold jersey from an online merchant which we would like to mention but probably can't—*yes, folks, it's the century rider!*

Is that you? Probably is. Because almost without exception, that's the kind of cyclist we're talking about when we're talking fanatical cyclists.

Now, it may seem to people immersed in cycling that the century rider is a cyclist not indeed worthy of definition, because we all know what one is, but just in case: A century rider is someone who trains for and participates in organized rides of 100 miles, which are called centuries, or rides of 100 kilometers, which are called metric centuries. The idea behind this pursuit is simple: Set a goal, the century event, and this serves as the excuse to ride a lot of hours every week in preparation for it! If you can find one thing wrong with riding a bunch of hours, there is probably something wrong with you.

The century rider can exist across a broad range of ages. You're likely to see people from 13 years old to nearly 90 years old on the roads of a century, but within this range of ages, the century rider takes two distinct forms. One form treats the century ride as if it were a race, and this person is very uptight about the exact time and order of finish. This person may do the same century 10 years in a row and judge his or her overall happiness or sadness for the year in terms of the time posted. This same person may ride through a full century course and at the finish, if the cyclecomputer registers 99.1 miles, this person will ride laps around the parking lot till the computer reads exactly 100.

The other form of century rider participates in the same event but doesn't give a hoot about elapsed time and stops at all the aid stations and enjoys the baked goods and free sports drinks and so on. Same event. Different mind-set. It is impossible to say which group has the more positive experience at the century. For one person's brutal experience is the same as another person's mellow day on the bike—and it doesn't matter, really, because most century rides raise money for charity, so the more people toe the line, as it were, the more money the ride raises.

We have to thank century riders, too, which means we're really thanking ourselves, because these tens of thousands of fanatical recreational cyclists are the good citizens who buy higher-end bikes and higher-end wheels and shoes and so forth, and the larger the market for these nifty items, the better these nifty items will be. And the cheaper they'll be, too! Tell me what's not to like about that?

THOUSANDS UPON THOUSANDS OF US

Behold the *naked man* in *Iowa*!

This is day 5 of RAGBRAI—the famous 7-day mass bike tour from west to east across Iowa—and while Dave is only one rider among the 10,000-or-so riders participating in this tour, he is not the only naked cyclist enjoying a skinny-dip in this wonderful, bubbling stream in Iowa farm country. It's midafternoon and shady here in the stream, with a few pleasant shafts of sunlight shining through the leaves and striking the glistening shoulders of cyclists, dozens of them. On the stream's banks: cycling clothing in heaps. Beyond that, against the trees and on the ground, there are bicycles by the dozens. On the road a hundred yards away rolls the longest steady stream of cyclists probably the world has ever seen—thousands and thousands of bikes on their way across Iowa. It's amazing. It's astonishing. Here in the

the RAGBRAI Rider: DAVE

1. So many bikes on the ground that you can hardly see the grass.
2. Riders coming.
3. Riders going.

89

stream itself, the way Dave's thinking, RAGBRAI might as well be Wood-stock. Dave loves it! He feels so free.

That's what he loves about RAGBRAI the most—the free feeling. He takes his time getting through the daily mileage, too, about 70 miles, because why hurry? Which is to say there are plenty of hammerheads on RAGBRAI, plenty of hard-core animal types on their bikes, people who rise at the crack of dawn and are done with their daily mileage before noon, but Dave says to hell with all that! He stays up late every night and drinks beer and meets people and macks on single women whenever he can find them. During the day, he rolls about 10 miles at a time and takes a break and then rolls 10 miles again.

And fancy that! At the end of a 10-mile segment, he has found a stream.

Near Dave stands another naked man—an older guy, very lean, with a wry grin.

The old guy asks, "How many years you been doing this?"

"This is my fourth year in a row," Dave says.

"I don't mean RAGBRAI," the older guy says.

"Well, what *do* you mean?"

"I mean, how long have you been a naturist?"

"A naturist?"

"You know, someone who is comfortable without clothes."

"You mean a nudist?"

The old guy grins and says, "Why, yes!"

Dave looks around and notices that in fact he and the older guy are the only people in the stream with their personalities hanging out. Everyone else is wearing a swimsuit!

Dave sinks into the water and feels an acute urge to get back on his bike and maybe pedal 20 miles before he stops the next time.

On the third day of the *AIDS/Life Cycle ride,* the 7-day AIDS research fund-raising tour that goes from San Francisco to Los Angeles every year, Amy rolls along in the pack and digs in her jersey pocket for an energy gel—and doesn't pay attention to the rider in front of her, who *brakes.*

She slams into his rear wheel with her front wheel and tumbles into the ditch. She sees her bike next to her, front wheel spinning, spokes glinting in the California midday sun, and she takes a long breath and moves her arms and legs to see if she's okay. She's not hurt too badly. Forty-seven years she's been around. She's borne children and been married and divorced a couple of times and has lost jobs and found jobs and lost friends to death and found new ones who love life. A little tumble on her bicycle can't stop her.

On the road, her friend Dale is yelling, "Amy, are you okay? Oh my God!"

Dale is in his forties, on the regular-beer side of a cycling build, and he's been Amy's best friend all through the training for this event and all through the event.

Amy says, "I'm fine." She sits up and can see blood dripping from her right knee. "I think."

Dale climbs into the ditch with her and asks, "Can you get up?"

Amy nods and extends her hand to Dale, who hoists her up and,

ouch, her knee's taken a decent whacking indeed. Dale helps her out of the ditch the rest of the way—each step is like a knife in Amy's knee—and she begins welling up with tears. She has raised sponsorship money for this event for months—almost $10,000, money that will go toward AIDS research—and, like so many other riders on this tour, she has lost her share of friends to AIDS. So for Amy, this isn't just a bike tour with friends and fun times camping in school gymnasiums. This is a seriously meaningful event, and for this reason, because she is in extreme pain and is thinking maybe her tour is over, she starts sobbing.

Dale holds her. "You'll be all right, dear."

Amy says, "I feel like I'm letting people down."

Dale attempts a joke. "You're not letting anybody down. You *fell* down."

Amy does laugh a wee bit and takes a couple of steps. Admittedly, these steps would be awkward with cycling shoes on her feet no matter if her knee were trashed or in pristine condition. She says, "I guess if I can walk, I can ride."

Dale says, "That's my girl!" He goes into the ditch and extracts Amy's bike and brings it to her and spins the wheels.

"The bike's okay," Dale says.

Amy takes her water bottle out of the bottle cage—odd: why didn't the bottle fall out in the crash?—and squirts some water on her knee. Not too bad. She'll survive. She has to survive. That's the whole point of this tour, to survive and raise money and awareness so more people can survive.

She slings a leg over the top tube of her bike and pushes off and clips her feet in the pedals and starts rolling. She pedals a few strokes—not too bad.

"Let's get our asses moving," Amy says.

Dale rides up to her and says, "You're an inspiration to me, Amy."

"You inspire me, too, Dale."

Thousands of riders are on the road, everyone here because they believe in the cause and believe, one day, there will be a cure for AIDS. Amy thinks, *Hell yes, this is inspiring.*

The Charity Rider

We have *century rides,* which most of the time
raise money for fine charities, and then we have
mass tour rides . . .

. . . which not only raise money but manufacture a sort of wholesome
Woodstock-on-wheels environment for cyclists in numbers of 500 or
1,000 or 5,000 or even 10,000 or more who roll 70 or 80 miles a day and
camp in fields or sleep on the floors of high school gymnasiums and in
general have the times of their lives. These mass rides attract a special
breed of rider, the type who enjoys the party that goes along with the
ride as much as the ride itself. And by "party," I don't mean staying up
late at the bar and doing shots of tequila (although some of that happens
on the overnights of these rides, too). Instead I mean the partylike atmosphere: Huge numbers of riders rolling down the road together for days
on end, people from different parts of the country making lasting
friendships, people falling in love, all of it happening in a two-wheeled
environment.

Now, it's true that in a party atmosphere of hundreds and even
thousands of cyclists, bad crashes sometimes occur, and sometimes
other nastiness occurs—and certain hard-core roadie types (the official
complainers of the cycling world) recommend staying as far away from
the carnage as possible. But really, the carnage doesn't exist, and you're
hard-pressed to find any cyclist with bad things to say about mass tours.

THE MOTHERS OF
ALL CENTURIES

Kira loves *punishment.*

Or that's what she tells people when they ask why she's out here every year riding the Hundred Hills of Hell Century. One hundred miles. Ten thousand feet of elevation gain. And that's just one of the events like this that she rides. She loves the rough centuries, the ones with climbing, the double centuries, the double metrics, the ones that ask more of the riders than merely rolling from a starting line to a finish line. Her friends at work—she teaches economics at a community college—don't get it. They ask, "Why don't you do something a little less extreme?" Or they say, "You're not in your twenties anymore." She wants to say,

_____ the Challenge Century Rider: KIRA _____

1. Expression is a combination of joy and pain. They want the ride to be *hard.*

2. Eyes up the road, looking into the next corner the way a hungry person looks at lunch.

"Yeah, I'm 45 years old, and my ex has the kids every other weekend. What do you want me to do on my weekends free? Hang out in a bar? Go golfing? Join a quilting society?" But she never says anything like this. She puts her energy into biking and not defending herself to people who don't understand what makes her tick.

So she's 72 miles into the Hundred Hills of Hell right now and is riding with a group of guys who seem to be approaching the ride with sanity—in other words, they stopped at the rest stop 10 miles back and filled bottles and peed and had a quick stretch. Lots of crazies on this ride don't stop at all, the idea being to get a faster elapsed time in the end, but the thing is, if your bottles are empty and you don't refill them, you will end up cramping and feeling like death. Sure enough, the group she's in passes other riders one after another—people whose bodies are almost out of gas, slumped over the handlebar, moaning through their pedal strokes.

Kari has no problems at the moment and lets her feelings be known. "I feel great, guys! How about you?"

There are four of them, all strangers to each other, and they all say, "Yep."

What she likes most about this group—and she notices this kind of thing week after week in these tough centuries—is that nobody treats her like the girl who can ride with the boys. They treat her like a cyclist who can ride with other strong cyclists. She doesn't normally approve of the word *empowerment,* on account of it's way overused, but what the hell: She feels empowered riding with these strong guys because, when you get down to it, this means she has amazing power, too.

One guy says, "This sure beats the shit out of golfing!"

Another guy says, "Or fishing. Can you imagine sitting on our asses in a fishing boat? On a day like this?"

Kira says, "Fishing? I don't even know what fishing *is!*"

Everyone has a good laugh, and Kira moves to the front of the group and steps up the tempo just slightly, just enough so it hurts but still feels good. There's more than 25 tough miles to go, and there's no point moping all the way to the end.

Is this punishment? No way. It's freedom.

For Andy, the Hundred Hills of Hell constitutes a benchmark for a whole year of *cycling* and *training* and *sacrifice*.

Everything in his life points to this event, the results of which indicate whether it's been worth it to show that kind of devotion to his sport. But right now, with 15 miles left to go, he feels like his entire year of cycling is flushing down the toilet. He's cramping everywhere, in the legs, the arms and neck and back, even his fingers. He doesn't have a drop left in either of his bottles. He is having difficulty breathing. Worse yet, he's acting like a jackass.

For the last 20 miles or so, he's been riding with the guy who's now 50 yards ahead of him on this long climb, but now the guy's powering away from Andy, looking smaller and smaller up the road with each passing pedal stroke. What happened, the guy was Mr. Happy-Go-Lucky, talking about what a fine event this is and what a nice day—going on and on about it—and finally, Andy couldn't take it anymore

---

the Dropped Challenge Century Rider: ANDY

1. Head down: Universal body expression that stands for "I'm blown."
2. Two miles from now, he will blame getting dropped on the extra weight in the saddle bag.

and said, "Listen, will you shut up and ride your bike? I'm riding for my personal best time here."

The guy was quiet for a moment, then said, "It's not a race, man. It's just a century ride with some hills in it. If you want to get in a race, why don't you get a goddam USA Cycling race license and start racing!" Then the guy rose from the saddle and stomped on the pedals and gapped Andy. Andy tried responding but couldn't. He was cramping in about 10 places at once.

Now Andy feels desperate and stupid and alone. Down the toilet. Dammit. He's put everything into this event: hired a fancy online coach and followed the coach's training regimen to a T, a regimen so brutal it made life lousy for months on end. He's been grumpy at home and over-tired and thirsty and hungry and whining about nearly everything. His wife's been sick of hearing about the Hundred Hills of Hell. His three kids have been tired of hearing about it. Even the people at work have asked him to please not mention the Hundred Hills of Hell or bicycles or bicycle parts or cycling clothing or ailments pertaining to cycling ever again. What's the reward for all this humiliation and sacrifice? Some random dude in a bike-shop jersey drops him with no problem—and with only a few miles to go? What a waste!

Andy yells, "Sorry, man. I didn't mean to be a jackass!" He hopes the guy will ease off the gas and ride with him again. But nothing. The guy keeps disappearing up yonder road without looking like he's putting any effort into it.

"Shit," Andy says.

Now a group of five cyclists passes him, and the last cyclist in line, a woman with long hair in a ponytail, says, "Excellent day for a ride!"

Andy doesn't agree. So he doesn't respond. A year wasted. Damn.

Challenge Century Riders

For some riders, a lot of a good thing is *never* enough.

Something beyond a mere 100 miles calls to challenge century riders not unlike the way the Sirens once called to Odysseus. These riders want the big one, the standard to which all other epic rides must compare.

What is the ultimate century? First, double the distance to 200 miles, and toss in 20,000 feet of elevation gain. That will about take the kick out of your legs, won't it? More commonly, the ultimate epic centuries—or challenge centuries, as they are known—do something on the order of 100 miles with 10,000 feet of climbing. And of course the challenge century wouldn't be truly epic without a truly epic name. Here are some classics: the Assault on Mount Mitchell, Mountains of Misery, Triple Bypass, the Death Ride, Horribly Hilly Hundred. Feel like signing up?

Now, if you were to ask a noncyclist at the mall for an opinion on the subject of a ride named Mountains of Misery, that person would say: "Nuts." But the truth is, most challenge centuries have waiting lists just to gain entry. It might be easier to obtain season tickets to the Green Bay Packers' home games at Lambeau Field than it is to get a bib number for the Death Ride.

Some of the participants in these events consider them to be a race, which isn't surprising, since the riders receive an elapsed time and results are posted in order of finish. But for racers in official racing categories, something like a challenge century is considered to be the equivalent of a regular recreational ride.

But if you ride 200 miles in 1 day, with 20,000 feet of climbing, does it matter if it's a race or not? Hell no. It only matters that 14 hours later, you cross the finish line with your hands on the bar and your head held high.

ROADIES

He is *moderately* famous, at least within the
world of *moderately* famous bicycle racers, and
we see him riding his bicycle in mufti—

not in his team uniform—which is proof he's moderately famous, because
only a moderately famous bicycle racer can afford to buy, at full cost,
cycling clothing not supplied by his team. While he's pedaling down the
road, however, you can't miss that this is a person who not only rides the
bike well but seems to belong on a bicycle. His pedal strokes are amazing
perfect circles, his cheekbones prominent under tight skin, his arms so
thin that any weight beyond the weight of a water bottle might stress his
biceps to the point of failure.

_____ the Male Pro _____

1. Pencil-thin arms.

2. Confident, smart-ass, completely relaxed expression.

3. Small jersey hanging loosely like an XXL T-shirt.

He's really tired. He's been racing almost nonstop for a couple of months, and the only reason he's out riding his bike today is because he has no choice. He needs the rest, but he needs to rest with his legs moving, something that doesn't even make sense to him, but he does it anyway because his entire life involves doing the proper thing in cycling. He's out for a 3-hour spinner, and when he's done with this, he's thinking about stretching for an hour and then loafing on the couch, with his legs elevated, and watching professional golf on the Golf Channel. In his view, there has never been a finer sport to promote viewer unconsciousness than golf, and unconsciousness is what he wants more than anything else in the whole world.

Someone rolls up alongside him now, a kid in his twenties wearing local bike-team kit and riding a midlevel race bike and clearly interested in chatting.

The kid takes the pro's left and wheels him up slightly, continually wheedling the pace faster by a tire length, which causes a strain and an unhappy dull ache to develop in the pro's legs.

The kid says, "Hey, man. You ride bikes much? You look like you could be pretty strong."

The pro says, "I ride a little bit. Yeah."

The kid asks, "You ever race?"

"Not today."

The kid doesn't seem to hear this. "Well, I race all the time. I'm a Cat 3. You know what that is?"

The pro used to be a Cat 3 about 12 years ago, when he was 15 and winning every race he entered, sometimes lapping the field in criteriums. Hell, he raced Elites at Junior Worlds how many times? But the pro doesn't feel like explaining it. The pro says, "I guess I don't know what a Cat 3 is."

"Oh well," the kid says. "Come to group ride at Big Ed's sometime. I'll show you some cool stuff about racing."

With that, the kid attacks down the street, carrying huge speed toward a stoplight, and the pro is surprised the kid is able to avoid slamming into cross traffic at the red light.

The pro chuckles. What a jackass! But he's glad the kid's up the road.

Bonnie is *broke.*

She wants to make that perfectly clear, that even though she has four bikes in her apartment and two closets full of cycling clothing and 10 pairs of cycling shoes, not to mention multiple helmets, sunglasses, gloves, tires, tubes, chains, spare wheels, spare cassettes, spare saddles, spare brake pads—gosh, is she forgetting anything?—all that bike stuff doesn't prove she has money. If anything, it proves that what money she's got, if she ever really had any extra, is tied up in her cycling. She didn't buy most of it, in any case, and the stuff she did buy she bought at a deep discount.

She also has one bookshelf crammed with medals and trophies and plaques and framed newspaper clippings, because that's the kind of rider she is: She wins. She's a professional cyclist but a professional in the amateur sense, because if you look at the other bookshelves in her apartment, you will see them crammed with novels and books of poetry and literary criticism and books on social theory and political theory

---

the Female Pro: BONNIE

1. From her desk, she can see her bikes, and from her bikes she can see her desk.
2. Overwhelmed expression.

and so forth. So aside from being a professional cyclist, she's also getting a PhD in English literature—specializing in 17th-century literature, thank you very much—and you don't get a PhD in English literature and you don't become a professional women's cyclist if you think you're going to have trunkloads of cash lying around your apartment when it's all said and done.

She has been standing in front of her refrigerator thinking about this and taking a few slugs of soy milk to calm her nerves. What else can she do?

Go for a ride, of course. And it doesn't take her long to suit up. Summertime. Midweek. She's in bib shorts and a jersey before you can recite the first 20 lines of Milton's *Samson Agonistes*.

She hears a knock at her door now and opens up, and her friend Alice is there.

Alice is not unfit, which is to say she's not fat or anything—she is actually quite beautiful, with flowing black hair and incredibly alert blue eyes—but Alice isn't a cyclist. She's a PhD student and has been one of Bonnie's officemates in the English department for the last few years.

Alice stares at Bonnie's cycling uniform and says, "Sorry. I didn't mean to stop by unannounced, but I was in the neighborhood."

"The ride can wait," Bonnie says. "Hell, everything else in my life can wait, for all anybody cares!"

Alice takes a long measure of Bonnie and cocks her head and says, "So what's really bothering you, Bonnie?"

"I'm two people."

"Who isn't?"

"I really *am* two people. I've got my bike life and then my English department life, and neither of those worlds cares about the other's existence."

Alice shakes her head and pats Bonnie on the shoulder. "Well, I care about you, Bonnie."

Bonnie says, "That's a comfort." She means that ironically and not ironically at the same time, but whatever the case, that pat on the shoulder has put Bonnie in a better mood. She smiles and blows out some air. "Sorry, Alice. I'm just so busy all the time."

Alice says, "I've got the cure for you. A bunch of us from the seminar are going to the Brewhouse tonight. Wanna come?"

Bonnie shouldn't drink beer. It collects on her ass like flies collect on cow shit. But the lit seminar people are so funny and crazy, and hanging out with them at the Brewhouse never fails to be the traditional graduate school proverbial bucket of laughs. Bonnie says, "I have to ride for a while now and do some work, so I'll just have to see."

"Come on," Alice says. "You know you'll have a blast."

"Okay then," Bonnie says. "I'll be there for one beer. But that's it."

Alice says, "You can do better than that."

Bonnie smiles. She *can* do better than that, and she will.

Dennis wants this training ride to *end* but at the same time wants to stay out for a while longer.

People on the sidewalks are gawking, no doubt because they can see plainly that he's no ordinary cyclist but in fact an amazing racer. Sure. People can't help but stare. People in the cars are staring at him, too, in his Big Ed's uniform, pedaling so perfectly and riding with such balance and such lightninglike speed. Like did you see how he dropped that skinny guy a few blocks back? The guy fell away from Dennis like a rock dropped off the Eiffel Tower. Now, that guy *looked* fast, but he was simply another slow guy who gives off the impression of having something special under the hood. Besides, the guy didn't even know what a Cat 3 is! Talk about clueless!

Dennis rolls up to a stoplight now—it's red—and he does a track-stand instead of putting his foot on the ground till the light turns green. He balances his bike with such ease, such grace. No wonder people watch him: He's an inspiration! Next to him is a pickup truck with two

---

the Category 3 Jackass: DENNIS

1. Sitting on top tubes, ultradorky way to look cool.
2. Looking around to see if anybody's staring at him.

---

guys in feed caps sitting in it with the windows open. The guy in the passenger seat is staring at Dennis.

Dennis plays the part of dignified cycling ambassador. He says, "Hey, man. How you doing?"

The guy in the pickup truck asks, "Why don't you just put your foot down and quit wobbling around like that?"

Dennis says, "Because I don't need to. I could balance like this for a full hour if I wanted."

"Looks like you're gonna fall on your ass to me."

"What?"

"Idiot," the guy says. The light changes, and the truck moves forward with traffic.

At first, Dennis can keep up with the truck, tucked in the truck's draft, 20 miles per hour, 25, 30, then he just can't manage it anymore. Dennis is fast but not as fast as a pickup truck. Oh well. He's ridden enough today anyway.

A few minutes later, Dennis carries his bike up the stairs to his apartment, which he shares with his girlfriend, Natalie, and he finds her sitting at the kitchen table reading a book and taking some notes for a college class in dialectical therapy or something like that. She doesn't look up when Dennis walks in.

"You wouldn't believe what just happened," Dennis says. "These two rednecks in a pickup truck called me a pussy for shaving my legs. And I totally chased them down to give them a piece of my mind. But they got scared and took off."

Natalie finally looks up. "You have the money for the utility bill? It's late by 3 weeks."

Dennis says, "If I win my race on Sunday, we'll be in high cotton."

Natalie has amazing brown eyes, almost black; sometimes it's as if Dennis can stare into them and see the meaning of the universe. Nothing is in those eyes now.

"Whatever," she says. "Keep up with the bicycle fantasy. I can tell it's really taking you places." She turns back to her homework, and Dennis doesn't know what to say.

How could she be living with him and not know how amazing he is at racing? He leans his bike against the wall and wanders in the direction of a hot shower and thinks, dammit, if he only had the money for the utility bill right now. Maybe he can sell one of his extra sets of wheels or something. Maybe that will get him by till the next race.

From this European-style Ford Econoline van, the *state road racing champion* is about to emerge.

He's been the champion for 3 years in a row and would have been the champ the year before that but was vacationing with his family in Italy at the time and couldn't convince his wife to come home early so he could be at the race. He was pissed because he was superstrong that year, too. But then again. Italy? It was *molto magnifico*.

The side door opens, and there he is: Bill. Forty-eight years old, 5 foot 10, 160 pounds. And here's his bicycle, a Pinarello Dogma with SRAM Red gruppo and Zipp 808 carbon tubular wheels—we're talking about eight grand worth of racehorse Bill's rolling out. The money he's spent on his body is impressive, too. He hired a very well-known online coach, not the low-level coaches sitting in cubicles at the online company's corporate offices; the real guy, the head honcho of the coaching

---

the Masters Sandbagger: Bill

1. Personal team tent (used only for bike races)
2. Euro-style van (used only for bike races)
3. Fancy race bike (used only for bike races)
4. Spare fancy race bike (used only for bike races)
5. Tools for all possible repairs
6. Old-man ass

---

company, has been personally coaching Bill. Plus he's hired the finest trainer at the local gym and the finest dietitian in town, and if some people think this is excessive, they need to think about Bill slaving his entire adult life to become a success in the mutual fund business. Why shouldn't he spend what he wants on his passion in life? He could be buying yachts—what's the big deal about a few bikes instead?

He's in his racing uniform—a custom-made skin suit that he always wears for events 1 hour and under, which today's criterium race will be. He's racing the Masters 40–49 Cat 4 race, and, barring a mechanical incident, he will probably win. So he's just standing there, as innocent as can be, and some of the guys in the parking lot start giving him grief.

"Hey, Bill," one of the guys says. "Are you gonna lap the field again this week?"

These guys are bike racers, too, obviously.

Bill says, "If you race harder, I won't drop you." He smiles to let them know he's kidding.

The guy says, "You should cat up, for crying out loud. You need to race with the big boys one of these years."

"Not gonna happen," Bill says.

The guy laughs, and the guy's buddies laugh, but this is not friendly laughing, really.

Bill is not stupid. He knows what's pissing them off. If he wins all the time in Category 4, the usual path suggests he should move up to a Category 3, but Bill has never been a person to follow the usual path. In his mind, the cat-up situation presents a serious problem. He's winning races now and is consequently enjoying himself a great deal, but if he moves up to the next category? No more winning. He won't be enjoying himself as much anymore. What's the point of having a hobby if you can't enjoy yourself? True, he's heard complaints, sometimes angry ones, that he's too fast for Cat 4, but if the officials don't actually force him to move up a category, why would he move up a category? Nobody can force him to move up a category, and if they were to try, he would sic a lawyer on their butts pronto.

So for now, he's having fun and not worrying about anybody else. That's the key to success for Bill.

He removes his stationary trainer from the back of the van and sets his bike on it and gets his iPod ready for his warmup sequence. Before the music comes up, he hears somebody say, "That guy is a total sandbagger."

Bill doesn't acknowledge this. He turns on his music and starts pedaling circles that look a hell of a lot like victory.

Road Racers

See that group of five small men, in *matching* spandex uniforms, with their *matching* road bikes arranged in a semicircle facing an even smaller man who sits on the top tube of his bike and gesticulates with his right hand as if he were issuing commands for the French army's invasion of Russia?

These are road racers, and when we use the term *roadies*, we generally mean this group of cyclists. This isn't to say that the century riders and the triathletes and so forth aren't riding road bikes, but the true roadie—the cyclist with a dictatorial manner and the desire not just to ride a bike on the road but to beat other cyclists in a race on the road—is a road racer. In the United States, not even 70,000 people hold road-racing licenses, which puts them in one of the smallest groups in cycling. They know this and feel therefore they are in an elite class of people in the sport. Any human being on two wheels who doesn't race is a "recreational" rider in the eyes of a road racer. A roadie despises triathletes. A roadie thinks poorly of old men on upright bikes. A roadie cracks jokes about fat people on bikes. A roadie believes that without roadies, there would be no cycling at all.

There are roadies who would object to this assessment, but then again, roadies will object to just about anything. If you are bored sometime, search the Internet for a road-racing message board (something that may seem like a thing of the past in the days of social networking, but trust me, the road-racing message boards are still there) and read through the discussion threads. Could be anything—tire choice, bike choice, race route, who's at fault for a crash, even the position of the sun in the sky—and the roadies will be bickering the subject to death. This bickering, it's worth pointing out, is oftentimes amazingly savage. Maybe this is because they race at high speeds in tight packs and have to yell at each other a lot to be safe? Probably not. Cyclists who aren't roadies almost universally believe that roadies behave the way they do because they are assholes. For proof of this: Call a roadie an asshole, and see if the roadie doesn't act like an asshole when he explains why he's not an asshole. Note that I use the pronoun *he* here, which isn't to say that there aren't female roadie assholes, but roadies are predominantly male, predominantly type A, predominantly the type of people who, were they to be taller and able to play lunch-hour basketball or weeknight softball, would take their involvement in their sport way too seriously.

Within roadies, there are countless subhierarchies, some of them determined by official racing categories on racing licenses (Cat 1 for pro and 2 for almost pro; Cat 3 for fast jackass; Cat 4 for fast beginner and old sandbagger; Cat 5 for slow beginner and medium-slow sandbagger), some of them determined by the time spent involved in the sport, but most of them determined by a simple, brutal fact: who is the strongest rider. Strength in racing, however, is not a matter of brute strength, really, because strength in cycling is not determined by actual power output but instead by speed and endurance, and because speed and endurance are a consequence of a rider's power-to-weight ratio, the strongest rider is often the smallest person in the group.

What the rest of the cycling world wants from roadies is a bigger, warmer heart. We can hear the response, too: "What the hell are you talking about? I have a *huge* heart!"

THOSE WHO CHASE
EACH OTHER
IN THE WOODS

Under the red roof of a portable tent, Frank is pedaling on a road bike affixed to a *stationary* bicycle trainer.

He has a couple of folding camping chairs in the tent, too, along with two Hardtail mountain bikes and some tools and a bike stand and a cooler. Frank is in his thirties, skinny, with muttonchop sideburns and a way of always looking like he's smiling even when he's not smiling. He clearly loves life and has not one ironic bone in his body.

Near him, a kid in his early twenties—also skinny—is pointing a digital camcorder at Frank and conducting an interview. The kid's name

the Fast MTB Racer: FRANK
1. Ultra lean.
2. Mutton-chop sideburns.
3. Fearless expression that could be construed as a smile.

is Ronnie, kind of a celebrity on this mountain bike race series because he puts up a video blog a couple of days after each weekend's events, along with results and links to pictures and other cool series-related stuff.

Ronnie is narrating an interview with Frank now: "Frank doesn't win *every* time but *almost* every time." Frank smiles and rolls his eyes in an aw-shucks way and chuckles and shakes his head and takes a drink from a water bottle.

Ronnie says, "So I'm just going to come out and ask you this. Do you think you're the strongest rider in the series?"

A drop of sweat falls off Frank's nose, and he watches it disappear into the grass under his front wheel. He says, "Nah. I love racing these courses. I love the people who make this possible. And I'm out here to have fun. Period."

Ronnie says, "You're awesome."

Frank keeps pedaling nowhere on his trainer and keeps smiling that smile that's hard to tell is a smile or not.

Ronnie says, "I can't help asking: What are you doing on a road bike?"

Frank smiles a real smile now and laughs. "This bike? This bike is my baby! I ride it all the time!"

"A mountain bike racer?" Ronnie asks. "On a road bike?"

"Most of the time, this is the bike I ride. Like tomorrow? I will be

---

the MTB Racer Web-Media Guy: RONNIE

1. Dogs off leash: This is what mountain bike racing is all about.
2. Kids playing Frisbee.

---

way too toasted and sore to take a mountain bike out on the trail. With
the road bike, I can spin easy for a few hours and recover and not worry
about concentrating on a technical trail. Know what I mean?"

Frank shifts to a higher gear and maintains the same pedaling rate,
revealing in his face the slightest suggestion of strain.

Ronnie asks, "You don't do road races, do you?"

"No offense to road racers, but road racing is an entirely different
situation than riding a road bike during the week to keep fit and recover.
Check out the friendly scene here today." Frank gestures to the cars and
trucks and vans that have formed a small groovy village here in the field
near this week's racecourse. People are mingling and talking and check-
ing out each other's bikes and playing catch with Nerf balls and playing
fetch with their dogs. "This is not an uptight scene. Racing bikes is fun
in this series. But the roadies? When they race?" Frank pauses and
shakes his head.

Ronnie asks, "What about the roadies?"

"Ah, nothing. It's bad karma to speak ill of our fellow cyclists."

RONNIE TAKES HIS camera gear from Frank's warmup tent and
heads down the row of vehicles parked on this grassy field, filming as he
goes. He stops occasionally to pan over the bikes, the people, the dogs,
the kids playing hacky sack. He approaches another tent and wanders in
and finds a man and a woman in spandex racing kit stretching on yoga
mats. He asks if they would mind being on his video blog this week.
They totally know who Ronnie is. Everybody in the series knows who
Ronnie is, and Ronnie knows everybody in the series. So the interview
is good to go.

He introduces his interviewees—Henry and Linda. They are in their forties and are very fit and very smiley and very positive.

Ronnie asks Linda, "How long have you been racing in this series?" Linda sits with perfect posture, with her legs straight in front of her, and she bounces them gently at the thigh. "This is my eighth year," she says.

"What do you like best about it?"

"Gosh," she says. "Can you feel the energy here? Everybody is *so* into it. *So* positive about it, too. I've tried a lot of other sports before getting into mountain bike racing—I ran, I played volleyball, softball, and so on—but the mountain bikers are by far the coolest people with the best vibe. You can literally feel the awesome vibe here each week."

Ronnie asks Henry the same question, and Henry shrugs. "Linda can do all the talking. I agree with everything she says anyway."

Ronnie laughs and asks Henry, "So how are you feeling about your race today?"

"Stoked," Henry says. Then he gets a more serious look on his face. "Okay, it's gonna hurt because that's racing, you know?"

Ronnie asks, "You fighting for the podium?"

"Fighting to keep my bike upright is more like it."

Linda says, "He crashed in our backyard just this week!"

They both laugh and Henry points to a bandage on the side of his left leg.

"Really stupid crash, too," Henry says. "I was riding a wheelie for Linda—trying to impress her, you know, because she likes that kind of thing." He elbows her and she smiles. "And I guess the wheelie was so good that I crashed into the flower bed."

"The flower bed is trashed, too," Linda says, "but looks like Henry's still upright and taking nourishment."

RONNIE'S LAST STOP on his video tour is his own vehicle, a classic white Chevy Astro van that he only drives to the races because the rest of the time he gets around town via bicycle. He pops open the rear doors and removes his Hardtail mountain bike and sets it up on a stationary trainer and sets up a camera tripod in front of his front wheel and mounts the camcorder on the tripod. Then he climbs into the van and reappears a couple of minutes later in racing kit and mountain bike shoes. He hops on the bike and leans forward and turns on the camera and starts pedaling and speaking into the camera.

"So here's my deal this week," he says. "I'm not going to do my usual sit-back-and-enjoy-the-race deal. Not this week. I'm going to go for it! Because that's why we're here, to go for it, right? I won't win or anything—not unless everybody in the field drops out before the end—but I don't care. I want to do the best I can today." He pedals a little harder for dramatic effect, then eases up. "A couple of announcements: big trail maintenance nights this week, Tuesday and Wednesday, in my town. I will totally be there with a strong back and a weak mind! Seriously, if you ride the trails, you owe it to the trails to help maintain them." He pauses and looks momentarily guilty. "Sorry. I'm off my soapbox now."

Ronnie reaches over his handlebar to the camera and turns it off and then begins pedaling with more energy. This is going to be a hard race today. He can't wait for the starter's whistle.

the Happy MTB Racer Couple: HENRY and LINDA

1. Happy expressions. This is way better than staying home and watching TV!

2. Enough bottles to stay hydrated for the entire race season.

3. Team flag, just in case someone wonders who they are.

The Mountain Bike Racer

Like the roadie, the cross-country mountain bike racer is a *competitive animal* who wants to participate in a legitimate race, sometimes with prize money (though there's usually not as much prize money as in the road world).

Also like the roadie, the mountain bike racer tends to be fit and regimented about maintaining fitness, because mountain bike racing is tough and hurly-burly and dangerous, even though probably not so dangerous as road racing, if only because the speeds aren't as high.

We have to dismiss consideration of the professional ranks here, which we don't do with roadies because even the lowest categories of road racers consider themselves to be professionals. Obviously, on the top end of mountain bike racing, there is ruthless competition and people willing to do just about anything to win. But after that, things mellow out considerably and become, as you might expect in a sport that takes place on dirt, much more down to earth. For the most part, for the rank and file in mountain bike racing—the regulars in the local XC series, the people racing the team 12- and 24-hour events, the people racing the dirt crits—the vibe is much closer to what we find in a triathlon, which is to say the vibe is a form of tipping the hat to each other and appreciating that even though they're racing against each other, they're really all racing together.

Yes, mountain bikers are happy to see each other at the races. They are encouraging to each other. They like each other. And when the time comes for them to head out into the woods with shovels and chainsaws and maintain the local trails, by God, even the strongest of mountain bike racers will be there to pitch in. True, they don't really ride together in the way that roadies ride together—mountain biking is by necessity a single-file endeavor—but the community sense among mountain bikers is unmatched anywhere else in cycling.

WHEN IN DOUBT,
CYCLOCROSS

One drizzly Sunday in late October—the last Sunday in October, in fact—Sally hammers her cyclocross bike down the final 100-meter stretch of the course, *the annual Halloween Cross.*

Everybody at the finish line—maybe 30 people—cheers at the top of their voices for Sally, not because she's winning the race or even finishing in the top 10, but because she is dressed up as the Statue of Liberty, with the face paint and the robes and the rays of ethereal sunlight projecting from her helmet. On her robes and every part of her: grass and mud.

---

the Cyclocross Women's Halloween Racer: Sally

1. Smiling, but her eyes are fixed on the first stretch of the course.
2. She jokes around like this at the starting line before every race. That's her game face.
3. Where's the beer?

She hears the cheers everywhere: "Lady Liberty! Way to rock it!"

She crosses the line and pumps her fist and rolls to a stop off the course where the other ladies from her race are collecting: Mrs. Claus, Pippi Longstocking, Mrs. Grinch, a few cabaret dancers, Little Red Riding Hood. The only woman who has worn regular racing kit for this race, Dolly, the series leader, is nowhere to be seen. She probably won. She always does. Sally is never there to witness Dolly's victory because she's always a couple of minutes behind at the end. But who cares? Sally does the best she can each week, and that's all that matters.

Sally strikes up a conversation with Mrs. Claus, whose real name is Jane and who looks great in the Mrs. Claus suit with the red leggings under her shorts. Mrs. Claus has mud spattered all over her costume and all over her face, too. In fact, all the costumes and riders at the finish line are spattered with mud and grass and are standing around in the light rain with the same casual attitude as if this were a sunny day in June.

"Oh my gosh," Sally says. "That must have been hard racing in that suit."

Mrs. Claus says, "I was overheating big-time. Especially on the run-up. Talk about brutal."

The run-up was brutal indeed, very muddy, very steep, and very long. Sally was dreading it every lap. She says, "What about the downhill after that? I can't believe I didn't biff coming down that thing."

Mrs. Claus agrees and asks, "How was it racing in *your* costume?"

"Really cold! Especially now!" She points to the goosebumps on her arms and shoulders to prove her point.

Just now, more cheering erupts from the finish line. The Girl in the Gorilla Suit crosses the line with one hand on her handlebar and the other clutching a can of Pabst Blue Ribbon.

Everybody's laughing and clapping, and the Girl in the Gorilla Suit rolls to a stop and pulls off her mask and her helmet and reveals herself to be Terry, who is usually not in last place. The gorilla suit must have hindered her progress. She takes a huge swig from her Pabst and wipes sweat from her forehead.

"What's the point of a Pabst hand-up," she asks, "if there's no way to drink it?"

The rain starts to fall a little harder, and not one person seems to care.

Mike thinks there might be two laps to go in the Cat 4 open race at Halloween Cross—that's the *beginners'* race—

and he should know for sure how many laps because the officials have a lap counter you can see when you go through the start-finish line on every lap. But when he went through that area a while ago, he was locked in a duel with Gene Simmons. Or maybe it was Ace Frehley. Who knows? And who cares? Mike was never that into Kiss back in the day. Nevertheless, a guy in a Kiss costume passed Mike at the end of the last lap and said something about rock 'n' roll or maybe it was about Detroit Rock City or maybe it was "They call me Doctor Love," and Mike is not too thrilled with the idea of getting his ass handed to him by a guy in a Kiss outfit.

Mike's costume reveals his classical lack of imagination: He is dressed as a middle-aged, out-of-shape cyclocross racer—the costume he wears every weekend in the fall. He wonders, if he were wearing a cool costume—dressed as a cop or a Viking or an Imperial Storm Trooper or a hot chick in a bikini (please, no!)—would the costume

Another Halloween Racer: MIKE

1. Even face paint can't cover up game face.
2. After this race, I'm going to become a poet.

change his personality enough to give him the strength and the resolve to chase down Gene Simmons and show him who's the boss?

Mike guesses he'll never know. He's bombing after Gene Simmons through a fun twisty wooded section of the course, and when Gene approaches a hairpin turn, he slows down and Mike draws near, and by the time Gene sprints out of the other side of the hairpin, he's dropped Mike just that bit more.

It's hopeless. Mike sucks at 'cross. A guy in a costume can whip his butt. Yet here Mike is, like every week, getting passed and chasing after the rock 'n' roll of somebody else's youth. Does this even make sense? Mike thinks it does, in a strange way that he can't explain adequately to anybody but other 'crossers.

At one corner, Mike yells, "Gene, you're killing me!"

Gene turns his painted face toward Mike and says, "It's the shoes, man."

Indeed Gene has silver Kiss shoes rigged somehow over his mountain bike shoes, and it's pretty funny. Mike has a laugh about it and falls even farther behind.

He's 20 yards behind Gene when they leave the woods and head into an open area in which one of the race teams—most of whom are drinking beer today and not racing—has placed a 10-foot length of 4-by-4 across the course. All these folks are in costumes—werewolves, Abe Lincolns, et cetera—and they're yelling, "Bunny hop, bunny hop!"

Gene bunny hops the four-by-four no problem, and everybody hollers with joy. Mike approaches and can hear the chant, and thinks about not doing the bunny hop and then thinks okay, he'll bunny hop it, and in the indecision, he doesn't lift his front wheel on time and ends up flying ass over tea kettle and landing hard on the ground. He hears the "Oooh" from everybody watching and gets up, and before he jumps back on his bike, he experiences a moment of profound spatial disorientation.

Abraham Lincoln is close by. Mr. Lincoln says to Mike, "Don't let that guy whip your ass. Chase him down!" Mike is stunned and unable to move. Abraham Lincoln? Why did he not say, "Four score and seven years ago"? Why not "A house divided against itself cannot stand"? Why not "In great contests each party claims to act in accordance with the will of God"? Why not the soulful gaze into Mike's eyes, the look of compassion and understanding and wisdom and everything wonderful and true about dear old Honest Abe? Abe yells, "Don't just stand there! Get your ass back on the bike!"

Mike snaps out of it and remounts and chases after Gene Simmons—he's around the next bend, somewhere beyond the part of the course Mike can see—and it crosses Mike's mind that he might be hallucinating all of this.

Cyclocrossers

Full disclosure: I, *Mike Magnuson*, author of this book, am a cyclocross racer.

In this sense, you must take it with the proverbial swig of Belgian Chimay when I say that cyclocross is the most totally awesome, most totally inclusive, most fun, most kick-ass, most A-1 wonderful form of bike racing on the face of God's green earth! For real! This is my considered opinion, and how the heck could I disagree with myself?

For those of you who don't know what cyclocross is (and it is always shocking to learn that not every cyclist knows), it is a form of bicycle racing on twisty mixed-surface courses—grass, mud, sand, gravel—usually between 2 and 3 kilometers per lap, and by rule, the racers are forced to dismount from their bikes each lap and hop over barriers or run up staircases or up hills so steep that it's quicker to run up them than to try riding up them. Cyclocross is a fall sport, meaning the deeper into the race season, the worse conditions can get (sort of like football is in the grandest of the grassy venues of NFL football). 'Cross is at its finest in rain and mud and snow and all manner of correlative slop, and oddly, the lower speeds and softer surfaces that result from these conditions make 'cross a relatively safe form of racing. When riders crash in 'cross, they almost always just pop right back up, unhurt except for pride, and start racing again. It's slippy. It's slidy. It's stupid. It's pointless. It's lunacy. And in Belgium, cyclocross is the national equivalent of NASCAR in the United States!

So why not give it a try?

I guess I should apologize for my lack of objectivity. Nevertheless, my question—why not give it a try?—is something you will frequently hear from 'crossers, because 'crossers tend to proselytize constantly in an attempt to convert people from another form of bike racing (or from no bike racing at all) to cyclocross. That's the discipline's vibe: We're doing this, and it's really cool! Come out and try it!

Consequently, 'cross is growing at a phenomenal rate in the United States, and among the many miracles it accomplishes is taking hard-core roadies out of their element and forcing them to participate in a mellow, encouraging form of racing. In other words, cyclocross impels roadies, who race 'cross in large numbers, to behave like mountain bikers.

See, in cyclocross, owing to the course and the conditions and the skill levels of the riders (this goes beyond fitness and into bike handling), the race field is strung out almost from the beginning of the race, meaning there is no peloton, no working together, no drafting (well, maybe there's a little), and what results for everybody is basically a solitary effort with other people around, sort of like a groovier, mellower, no-swimming version of triathlon except contested on a messy, twisty course, with lots of dismounts and basically no hope of victory!

As with the top end of mountain bike racing, the top end of cyclocross is serious and competitive, and there are world-class athletes trying to whale the tar out of each other on the courses week in and week out during the season. But for most of the people involved in 'cross, the event is all about the experience of racing—tough and slow—for 35th place out of a field of 45. Like Vince Lombardi once said, "You have to win the war with the man in front of you." And that's what happens in 'cross: There's somebody in front of you and somebody behind you, and in the end, all that matters is how you competed against those people. It's fun. It's humbling. It's a way for people to have fellowship. And on Halloween, the 'crossers race in costume!

THE LEGEND OF
RANDO

Adam is *62 years old* and pedaling steadily down the road, even more steadily than he did 30 years ago, when he was at the top of his racing form, which means that maybe he's at the top of his racing form now?

He's not riding as fast as he used to, this is true, but he can ride longer by factors of hundreds.

There's nobody else on a bike near him right now, at least not that he

---

the Rando: ADAM

1. Expression is a combination of 1,000-yard stare, lifelong determination, and crusty wiseacre with something to say.

2. Panniers holding extra tubes, extra tires, an extra chain, spare cable, spare batteries for the lights, multiple CO_2 cartridges for tire inflation, three ham sandwiches, six ClifBars, one container of Pringles, extra socks, extra shorts, extra jersey, a rain jacket, arm warmers, leg warmers, and two tubes of Bengay.

3. Handlebar bag holding maps, wallet, and emergency contacts, on which he has listed himself.

can see, and the only way you could tell he's participating in an event is by the number pinned on the back of his jersey. His bike setup—huge saddlebag, map case on the handlebar, mirror on his helmet—gives off a decidedly old-man-out-for-a-joyride impression, but at Adam's age, he doesn't give a damn what impression he gives; he can do the talking with his legs. He's three-quarters of the way through his final qualifying event for the Paris-Brest-Paris event, a 1200-K self-supported half-race/half-self-test that is held every 4 years. This qualifying event is 600-K, and he has 40 hours to complete it. He will finish well under 40 hours, too, and this includes sleeping 6 hours in a hotel last night!

Up ahead, he sees a gas station/convenience store—seems like it has miraculously appeared in the curve of the road—and he panics. Is this the checkpoint on the route? Does he have to stop at this store, or is it the next one? But it's all fine. He sees a sign: "Randonnée Checkpoint." That means he's on course and on the way toward tall cotton.

He rolls into the lot, leans his bike against the convenience store wall, and removes his helmet and his gloves, which he chuckles about because it proves his mind is still alert: He read in *Bicycling* magazine once upon a time that a cyclist should always remove helmet and gloves before entering a place of business. He still remembers that article, and he's been riding his bike for more than 30 hours. This bodes well for his fitness.

When he enters the store, the wave of air-conditioning is so strong he feels like he has jumped into a cold mountain spring, and he shivers.

He is cheerful anyway and approaches the cash register. He digs out his Randonnée card from his jersey pocket and presents it happily to the rather substantial woman behind the counter.

"I'm with the Randonnée," he says and smiles. "Will you punch my card, please?"

THE LEGEND OF RANDO

"Not till you take a shower, hon," she says, and winks.

Adam likes this. He's not too old to flirt with a big young girl with tattoos and a nose ring. And you tell him all his miles on the bike aren't worth it? He keeps conversation on the up-and-up, though. He asks, "A lot of riders come through already?"

"Since my shift started," she says, "there's been about 10 of you. So how many miles are you riding?"

"Six hundred kilometers."

"How many miles is that?"

"Just shy of 375."

"That would hurt my butt so bad it might fall off."

"It's not as bad as you think," Adam says. "After a while, you can't feel anything at all."

"Maybe I should give it a try." She gives her gum a couple of ferocious chews and smiles.

Adam wants to tell her he's been riding bikes his whole life—used to be a fast road racer, used to be a cross-country touring rider, and now he's a randonneur—and that without cycling, his life would have no meaning whatsoever. He wants to say that here he is, in his sixties, still fit and still strong and still going after it, whatever *it* is, and if she were to start riding bikes seriously right now, she would have such a great future. But Adam's not a cycling priest. What she does with her life is her business, not his.

So instead, Adam buys an almond Snickers and some Gatorade and thanks the woman so much for punching his card.

She asks, "What's your name, anyway?"

"My name," Adam says, "is Rando." Then he winks at her and goes back outside and gets on his bike.

The Randonneur

First, you need to digest the name *randonneur* and figure out what it means.

A randonneur is a person who competes in Randonnées, and a randonneur cannot participate in a Randonnée without first competing in a prerequisite series of brevets (pronounced brew-vays). You are confused? This is understandable. But if you meet a randonneur in person, please don't mention your ignorance of the randonneuring pursuit. A randonneur, you see, is a cyclist who rides incredibly long distances without the support of a crew. The classic North American Randonnée is the annual Boston-Montreal-Boston (currently on hiatus for logistical reasons), 1,200 kilometers in length, and riders have to finish this in 90 hours. The most famous Randonnée in the world is Paris-Brest-Paris, also 1200-K. This was really the first major race in the history of bicycle racing, first run in 1891, and would probably have gone on to be the most famous bicycle race in the world had not a newspaper come up with the idea for the Tour de France and promoted Tour de France more effectively.

To enter a Randonnée, in any case, a person needs to participate in a series of four brevets, distances of 200, 300, 400, and 600 kilometers, and these must be completed within prescribed time limits before a person can toe the line at the Randonnée. Key to this process is that you have to be certified as completing these brevets in the same calendar year as the Randonnée in question. Is this tough? Are you freaked out by this whole idea? Or, like me, do you process the number and think, *Yeah, I would like to do that?*

So the process is complicated, but it's not nearly as complex as the sheer willpower, tenacity, and brute endurance required of the randonneurs themselves, who do this not because they want to beat one another but because they want to see what's in themselves, what limits they have mentally and physically. All cyclists—from the greatest pros to the meekest beginners—owe respect to the randonneurs.

THE HAPPY
WANDERERS

Jim and LeAnn—schoolteachers by trade and in their early thirties with no children—have traveled *huge distances* on their bikes in the last few years.

One summer, they bike-packed all the way across the United States, from San Francisco to Philadelphia. Another summer, they rode the entire Continental Divide Trail north to south. For part of another summer, they rode around Lake Superior. The rest of the time, they're out touring basically every weekend for at least one overnight and for a few nights longer than that, if possible. They love touring, the whole process, packing their gear in their bob trailers and taking out a map and making a route and making an adventure of whatever they may encounter

the Touring Cyclists: JIM and LEANN

1. Stuff spread out on table, signifying home is anywhere you can make it feel like home.
2. Steel bike with panniers and handlebar pack and fenders: The old school is still the best school.

along the way. Touring, they like to say, is a way to travel into a life.

This Sunday morning, they're awake on the second day of a 3-day leg-loosener tour, having spent last night in this picnic shelter in this small-town park. They had been aiming for the big state park that's about 20 miles from here but had to abort the mission when a huge thunderstorm blew up from out of nowhere. They rode out the storm in this shelter, but once the rain stopped, night had fallen, too dark to get back on the bikes, so they decided to stay.

Now they're sitting at the shelter's picnic table and drinking coffee they brewed on their MSR stove, peering at the map and getting their minds around where they're going to ride today.

LeAnn says, "We can easily make it to this town here—that's 60 miles maybe?"

"At least," Jim says. "We can go longer than that if you want."

A squad car pulls up to the shelter and comes to a cautious stop, and a portly officer steps out and walks slowly their way.

LeAnn says, "Morning, officer. Beautiful day!" She usually talks first. She can't help it. She's a cheery, outgoing person.

Jim chimes in, too, because he's damned cheerful, too. "It's a regular postcard out this morning!"

The officer is pasty-skinned and seems a bit distracted, as if an invisible 20-pound anvil of misery rests on the top of his head. He asks, "Where you from?"

LeAnn explains that they're from not too far away and that this is a short bike tour for them but they love to tour for weeks and weeks if they have the opportunity to do so. She mentions how they rode across the United States one summer and how much they enjoyed that and how if the officer ever got the urge to ride across the country, he should go for it because it's such a powerful experience.

The officer listens carefully and doesn't seem amused. "So you have everything you need, right here on your bicycles?"

Jim rises and shows the officer their gear: the bob trailer, the cook stove, the groovy camping-style espresso maker, and so on.

The officer soaks it in and asks, "What do you do when the weather's bad?"

"Last night?" LeAnn says. "We prayed that we would make it through the storm alive!"

Jim says, "Oh my gosh, that was a rough one."

"Found this shelter in the nick of time, too," LeAnn says.

The officer furrows his brow and rests his hands on his hips, his right hand near his sidearm. "Then you stayed the night here?"

Jim says, "Didn't have another choice."

The officer says, "For your information, we have an ordinance against camping in the municipal parks."

LeAnn explains the situation with the state park, the 20 miles, and how by the time the rain stopped and the wind died down, night had set in and no way could they have safely kept pushing on in the dark. "Definitely no other choice, officer," she says.

Jim starts to say something, but the officer lifts a hand to indicate he's heard enough. The officer gives Jim and LeAnn each a hard, soul-searching stare and succeeds in scaring the crap out of both of them.

Finally, the officer says, "Seems like no harm's been done. Maybe in the future, you can have better contingency plans for bad weather."

Jim says, "Yes, sir."

LeAnn says, "Yes, sir."

The officer excuses himself and says good-bye and walks slowly back to the squad car. He backs out and drives away.

When he's out of sight, LeAnn grabs Jim's hand and says, "Holy shit! I thought we were gonna get arrested."

"Totally," Jim says, "and did you see his hand near his gun? What was he going to do? Shoot us for riding out a storm in his little park?"

"Just when you think you've seen everything," LeAnn says.

A few weeks later, they have friends over for dinner, and after a few bottles of wine, LeAnn and Jim tell the story with Jim acting out the part of the cop. Their friends laugh so hard they have tears in their eyes because it's one of the funniest stories they've ever heard.

"That's why we love touring," LeAnn says to her guests. "You never know what amazing story you'll ride into next."

The Touring Cyclist

Purity *is* what purity *does.*

A person has a bike, some panniers or a bob trailer, plus the desire to learn exactly what the word *yonder* means. To ride across the United States! To ride the entire Continental Divide or around Lake Superior or from Minneapolis to New Orleans—because why? Because why not? Because touring is an epic way to take a vacation. To tour is to explore, and to explore—for touring riders and maybe for all cyclists—is to discover the true essence of the sport of cycling, because exploring is one of the reasons we ride bicycles in the first place. Bicycles transcend transportation from place to place. They are a way to transport between states of mind.

The touring cyclist, therefore, is the guru of cycling, the person to whom a trip on two wheels is more than a sport. A touring cyclist is an adventurer. In a sense, the touring cyclist is at once a loner, a person who tucks inside the mind and rides 80 miles into a headwind in South Dakota and a person who enjoys the company of strangers during stops in the day and stops for the nights. A touring cyclist is also the most resourceful of all cyclists, because you never know what will happen on the road or trail far from home and far from the comfort of the local bike shop.

Think about this: Who has not seen a touring cyclist, fully loaded with panniers or a bob, passing through town, and not wanted to ask, "Hey, where you riding from? Where you headed?" The touring cyclist is used to these questions, too, and is handy with the answers. The touring cyclist will never complain to noncycling strangers, which means they are unique in all of the sport of cycling, because, at least to others, they have nothing but good things to say.

THE
COMMUTERS

Michelle *does indeed* own an automobile.

She likes to make that perfectly clear to people, that if she wants to drive somewhere, she can and will and regularly does. She drives to the mall, for example, or drives to the movies with her friends or home to her parents at least 1 weekend a month. So when you see her riding her bike on the way to campus, let's just say she believes bike commuting is the quickest way to get to class and back home. Her apartment is about a mile and half from campus. If she were to drive this distance and find a place to park and then walk all the way to the building where she needs to be, it would take twice the time it takes to ride to school and lock her bike in a rack and go to class.

_____ the Commuter: MICHELLE _____

1. Bell. Fun to ring when she rides by her friends.
2. Happy expression. This isn't transportation; this is fun!

She's riding her hybrid to class now and trying to enjoy the ride instead of thinking about the class because it's a tough class that she hates: Statistics 420: Multiple Regression Analysis, which sounds like a class on serial killers but isn't. She's not riding fast and not working up the slightest sweat and merely enjoying the wind in her face and the sunshine and the fresh air.

She stops now at a red light and puts her feet on the asphalt and looks around and sees a police car driving by with the cop inside, a man about the age of her dad. She waves at the officer, and the officer waves back.

When the light turns green and she rolls through the intersection, she feels a presence next to her and turns her eyes to the left. There's a good-looking guy on a mountain bike riding just off her left shoulder! He seems to be about her age—22 years old—a clean-cut guy, rugged jaw. He's wearing a helmet, too, which signifies to Michelle that he's responsible about riding his bicycle.

She takes a risk and speaks to him.

"Nice day," she says.

"That it is," he says and pulls up next to her and rides alongside. "You always wave to cops?"

Michelle laughs, or is it a giggle? This guy was really paying attention! She says, "My mom told me to wave at policemen when I was a little girl, and now that I'm a grown woman, I'm still waving!"

"Makes sense," the guy says, "if you say so."

He's riding with a book bag on his back, so Michelle naturally assumes he's a student.

She asks, "What are you studying at school?"

"Nothing this semester," he says. "I'm working at a job for a while."

"Doing what?"

"IT stuff. 1 fix computer networks."

"And you ride your bike to work?"

"Trying to reduce my carbon footprint," the guy says. "It's the right thing to do."

Michelle says, "Right on!" And she tells him her name and what year she's in at school and a bunch of other stuff. He says his name is Ned and that he rides 4 miles to work each day and loves the fresh air and the clear head that comes with it. Michelle can't believe how well they're clicking.

After a few more blocks, Michelle has to turn toward campus, which she tells Ned. They both slow a moment and have one of those awkward moments when Ned is probably supposed to ask her for her cell number. He doesn't.

He says, "Nice to meet a fellow bike commuter. See you again sometime."

Michelle says, "Sure."

She watches Ned pedaling away and thinks, *Shoot, I'll bet he already has a girlfriend.*

A few blocks later, Ned feels a liquid blob of molten-rubber shame sinking from his shoulders all the way to his shoes *spinning* his bike pedals.

A semester off from school. Biking to work. Telling pretty girls it's about the carbon footprint. What a load of crap! He picks up his pace to vent frustration, forces his legs down with each stroke, almost with anger, but the frustration passes. It always does when he's on his bike. His bike is like a two-wheeled happy pill. Besides, what else is he going to do? Ned has no choice but to ride his bike everywhere he goes.

See, what he couldn't tell that nice girl is that the reason he's riding to work and not driving is because his driver's license has been suspended for a full year because he's had the profound misfortune of receiving not one but *two* citations for Operating a Motor Vehicle While Under the Influence—in fact, the same cop arrested him for drinking and driving two Saturday nights in a row! Of all the crappy luck!

No point in griping about it. He just has to suck it up and live

---

the Commuter: NED

1. Heavy duty lock. If his bike gets stolen, he can't get to work. Period.
2. Helmet has a visor, but he's not really sure why.
3. Cute girl noticing him.

through the suspension, and when it comes to pass that he meets a pretty girl riding a bicycle, when he knows damn well she wants him to ask for her number, he can't ask for her number because then he would have to explain the OWI situation and the license suspension, and what would she think of him then? She would think he's a no-account drunk—that's exactly what she would think.

But Ned's not a no-account drunk. He happened to go out drinking two weekends in a row and happened to get nailed both times, but those were freak, isolated incidents.

Or then again, maybe he was getting out of control with the whole party lifestyle. He's out of the party life now, for whatever that's worth, and he has to admit that with each successive week commuting, he feels happier about life in general. He's lost a few pounds. He's sleeping better than he has for years. When he's not riding, he finds himself thinking about his bicycle—the feel of the road and of the sun and of the air faintly whistling through his helmet. And get this: Both days last weekend, for no good reason other than that he thought it would be cool, he went on 3-hour rides on the bike path. And he's been making increasingly frequent trips to Big Ed's Cyclery and looking at new bikes.

Ned can tell you one thing for sure: When he does get his driver's license back, he's going to keep on biking. No doubt of it.

Now he feels a presence near him. It's Karl pulling alongside. Ned seems to bump into Karl almost every day on the ride to work—a guy in his forties, usually wearing a dress shirt, except on Fridays, which are casual days in Karl's office. Today, Karl's wearing the shirt and tie and got the dress pants, and he's riding a really cool-looking steel bike with fenders and a rack that holds his briefcase.

Karl says, "I hear there might be rain on the way home."

Ned says, "That's what they're saying."

Funny thing that's happened since Ned started riding a bicycle everywhere: He's an expert on the weather now, the kind of person who checks the forecast on the radar obsessively on his computer all day. Every cyclist Ned's bumped into is the same way—they are all like farmers on two wheels, always jabbering about the weather!

Ned asks, "Do you ride your bike when you're not commuting?"

Karl says, "Sometimes. Not too often, really."

"Do you have to ride your bike to work?"

"What do you mean?"

"Do you have to? Like, do you have no other choice but to ride to work?"

Karl thinks about this. "I do," Karl says, "but only because I've been riding to work for so many years I would think something was wrong if I didn't."

"That's cool," Ned says.

They roll along and don't speak for a while, but there is no awkwardness or discomfort.

Karl says, "Tomorrow and Friday are supposed to be midseventies and sun."

"Low temps in the fifties. Could be cold on the way in to work."

"Could be," Karl says.

Ned smiles. He likes the way bike people talk with each other. He can foresee lots of good things coming from this.

Karl thinks Ned is a *good* kid.

When Ned makes his turn, Karl tells the kid to have a great day, then rolls a few more blocks toward where he works, the Pig, which is his secret code name for the insurance company where he's a statute analyst. He's been working there for 20 years and has been bicycle commuting—6 miles each way—for almost the entire 20 years. He's missed some stretches owing to the weather or a broken-down bicycle or the simple wrongheaded desire on occasion to hop in a car and drive to work like everybody else. Still, this commute is an aspect of his life he's certain he couldn't live without, if only for the complete solitude from the world of professional hassles: no phone calls, no e-mails, plenty of fresh air and happiness.

He rolls into the company's parking lot at quarter till nine, and the lot is mostly empty. In 5 minutes, cars will come tearing in from what seems like all directions. Once nine o'clock hits, the insides of the building will be teeming with what Karl likes to call "microscopic life,"

---

the Commuter: KARL

1. Top-notch touring bike, with fenders, suitcase, and bar-end shifters.
2. Facial expression that says, "I am not thinking about my job."
3. Helmet, proof of intelligence.
4. Light, just in case something goes wrong on the way home.

because it lives and it moves, but it doesn't spend too much time thinking. Karl, of course, is proud of the fact that he can think, and he believes bike commuting has helped him to be the kind of person who can think.

He parks his bike at the rack. He's the only employee who ever uses it. He notes with some satisfaction that the management agreed to move the rack under one of the building's concrete overhangs—this way, his bike stays out of the sun, and if rain falls, the bike stays dry. Now he locks the bike with a U-lock and takes the strap off his right pant leg and takes the bungees off his briefcase and exhales very deeply. Okay, he thinks. Game face.

He hears his name now, spoken by a gruff lady's voice. Millie. An actuary. She's been with the company since the final days of the American Revolutionary War and is relentlessly skeptical of anything in this world that strikes her as out of the ordinary.

Millie says, "I've been meaning to ask you about your bike for quite a while now."

Twenty years? This is the first she's going to mention his bike?

"It's a steel frame," Karl says, "and it's been a great bike so far. I've had this one for 2 years now."

"I don't mean your bike itself. I mean, why do you ride your bike to work? Do you not have a driver's license?"

Karl takes a moment to calculate a polite response. "I *could* drive, I guess, but I enjoy riding to work. It clears my head so I can concentrate better at my desk."

Millie shakes her head in a dismissive way. "Why don't you just go to the gym?"

"Because I enjoy my bike."

"What do you do when it rains?"

Karl's mind races with nasty things he might say to her, how he could give a damn about her rheumy eyes staring at him and her puffy face wagging in disapproval of him, but he lets it go. He'll vent his frustration later, on the bike ride home. So he says, "When it rains, I get rained on."

Millie says, "Sounds stupid."

Karl says, "It *is* stupid. But I enjoy it anyway."

He nods to her and walks with his briefcase toward another long day working inside the Pig.

The Bike Commuter

Next to the touring cyclist—which we have to phrase in a sort of *cleanliness-is-next-to-godliness* way—the commuting cyclist is the person all cyclists most want to be.

For illustration, let me ask a stupid question, rolling my eyes when I ask it: Have you ever heard of bicycle commuting? Your response will be, Have you ever heard of oxygen? And I will say, Then why aren't you commuting to work every day? Or why are you driving your car three-quarters of a mile to the liquor store to buy a six-pack of Pabst? See, the bicycle is designed to transport a human being from one place to another. Like, duh? So how come most cyclists—in the United States, at least—consider bikes to be a recreational item and not a mode of transportation?

You would have to ask a real bicycle commuter for that answer, and, sadly, except on college campuses, the presence of real commuters is scarce indeed. Even the toughest weekend cyclists—roadies, mountain bikers, winners of multiple races—drive cars to work and to the store and to the department store and to the daycares and the schools their children attend. Cyclists like to ride bikes for kicks but not for getting somewhere, and, of course, all serious cyclists feel incredible guilt at not riding everywhere they need to go (except for certain hard-core roadies who feel that when they're not training or racing on a bike, they should be at complete rest). Consequently, the sad truth is that the true bicycle commuter is cycling's equivalent of a bald eagle soaring over the streets of, say, Chicago in the middle of winter.

It's not easy for the commuter to manage the routine of getting to and fro, especially if this person works in a professional environment that requires attire other than sweaty bicycle clothing. We're talking about leaving earlier for work, finding a way to get cleaned up and changed upon arrival—not to mention stockpiling clothing at work— then reversing course at the end of the day and pedaling the long way home. And what happens in the rather likely event of rain? Sleet? Earthquake? Alien attack during rush hour? At minimum, the commuter will be inconvenienced, and in the case of alien attack, the aliens might befriend the commuter because the commuter is so entirely foreign to our culture.

It's a nightmare all around (aliens notwithstanding). But this doesn't deter the commuter, because the commuter operates on a commitment to human-powered motion, which is good for both the environment and the rider.

THE MASS IS
CRITICAL

On Thursday night, Athena and Cameron,
girlfriend and boyfriend, in their twenties, are
unlocking their bikes outside a coffee shop.

"How much time we got?" Athena asks. She's much shorter than Cameron and is wearing hemp capri pants and an olive-drab T-shirt, and when she talks, she has a way of making cleaverlike gestures with her hands.

Cameron says, "No worries. We'll get there on time." He's in jeans and is wearing a Che Guevara T-shirt.

Athena says, "We really need to make a statement tonight."

"We will," Cameron says. "I heard we're going to ride through the mall tonight."

---
the Critical Mass Riders: CAMERON and ATHENA
---

1. Had Che Guevara lived to see Critical Mass, he would have insisted everybody wear a helmet.

"*Through?*"

"Yeah. Just open the doors and all of us will ride from one end of the mall to the other."

Athena asks, "You think we can get arrested for that?"

"What are the cops gonna do? Arrest a hundred people at once for riding bikes through a mall? Cops don't have that kind of manpower. That's why it's called Critical Mass, because we're massed together and can totally make a statement about the need for bikes and not get in legal trouble for it."

Athena says something about how cool that is and they start riding toward the city center, where the Critical Mass ride forms every Thursday night. They ride side by side in the road, almost in the middle of it, and they're totally not worried about motorists getting irritated with them.

Like now. A man in a Hyundai is behind them and can't get past them because they're taking up the full lane. He starts honking.

Cameron says, "Can you hear something? Because I can't hear *anything.*"

Athena laughs.

The guy behind them sticks his head out the window and yells, "Hey, assholes! Quit taking up the road. Use the goddam bike lane!"

Athena says, "You're not going to flip him off, are you?"

"Why bother? Our *actions* are flipping him off."

They reach a stoplight now and stop near the curb. The Hyundai pulls up next to them, and the man rolls down his passenger-side window and leans toward it. He's skinny, with short hair, and looks like an athlete. He says, "If you people are going to ride like idiots, you at least could wear helmets."

Then he drives off quickly when the light changes.

Athena asks, "What did he say?"

"I have no idea," Cameron says. "I never listen to people in motor vehicles."

Critical Mass Riders

A *commuter is one thing,* a great and admirable thing, and quite another thing is the rider who gets around on bicycles because it demonstrates a commitment to *sustainable* living,

to streets where bicycles can pass safely, with bicycle lanes and proper signage, streets free of redneck assholes in pickup trucks trying to run you off the road. All cyclists want safety and bike lanes and respect from people in motor vehicles. We will not budge on that one bit.

Critical Mass, therefore, is a popular form of group protest wherein cyclists do exactly what their name suggests: They mass together and protest the lack of respect to cyclists shown not only by drivers of motor vehicles but by the city planners who don't accommodate for regular cycling in their communities. In smaller areas, obviously the mass is smaller; in larger areas, the mass is bigger. And in this mass they literally take over the streets. They stop traffic; they block intersections; they draw attention to themselves in any way they can because they want the public to know that bicycles are here and that bicycles deserve the same space on the streets that automobiles have. They do not care about whatever inconvenience they may cause to the motorists during the Critical Mass ride, because look at the inconvenience the motorists cause to cyclists!

Nobody—cyclist or motorist—will deny that the Critical Mass movement has a valid point. If we want to conserve fossil fuels, if we want to reduce carbon emissions, we need to find methods of transportation other than the single-passenger automobile that is as common to the streets of the United States as horseflies are to the backs of horses. So there is no opening for debate here.

The methods the Critical Mass movement uses, however, are a cause of continuing controversy, mostly because Critical Mass pisses motorists off and in turn pisses law enforcement off. Some folks wonder whether an undeniably correct idea (that bikes are necessary and need a place) is undermined by the undeniably obnoxious manner in which Critical Mass promotes it. And the non–Critical Mass riders sometimes end up taking shit from motorists because of Critical Mass.

Most cyclists, deep down, support Critical Mass and what they're up to. Many cyclists who support them, like me, wish more of them would wear helmets during their protests, because hundreds of unhelmeted cyclists taking to the streets to promote a better world for bicycles, well, just seems plain stupid. Other than that, yeah: Fight the power! Ride a bike!

WE CAN FIXIE THIS

On the velodrome track, before her first interval, Heidi feels *philosophical*.

It occurs to her that if she had chosen a more spiritual path in life, she might have been an excellent monk. Look at her life: She goes to bed every night before 9:00 and gets up every morning at 4:30 so she can get to the gym when it opens at 5:00. At the gym, she lifts weights and does muscle conditioning and plyometric routines for at least an hour, usually a bit longer than that. You want to know the reason she comes to the gym this early? Because she's a 5-foot-3-inch, 125-pound, 29-year-old woman, and if that's who you are, you need to use the free weight area in the gym long before the muscle-minded weight-room jackasses show up and commence hoisting more weight than they should, because

_____ the Track Racer: HEIDI _____

1. Head slightly cocked to make up for the track's angle.

2. Full concentration.

3. Body is solid muscle.

when they're not staring at themselves in the mirror, they absolutely will hit on a woman who looks like Heidi. It's not her fault. It's theirs. It's gross, too. She's there to improve her strength for racing bikes on the track, not to set herself up romantically with some meat-for-brains who enjoys flexing his biceps in front of a mirror.

After the morning session at the gym, she spends her day putting out metaphorical fires at the logistics firm where she is in charge of making sure semitrucks loaded with groceries and electronic merchandise arrive safely, and on time, at distribution centers all over the country. In logistics, the old saying is "Everything goes wrong, all the time." Her job is to make everything right. All day, she wishes she were out training.

Therefore, after that kind of long day, when she arrives at the velodrome and suits up and begins taking a few slow laps around the track's lower lip, she can't help thinking that her life is about as regimented as it could be: gym, work, track, dinner, bed. A monk's life. On weekends, she usually races. That's it. That's not a very fancy life. Oh well. She's not complaining. Deep down, she wouldn't want a fancy life even if it were available to her.

The track's never fancy, either. She rides around it. That's what you do on a track. Endless ovals. She races the various events, too—scratch race, miss 'n' out, time trial, pursuit (when they have it)—and at no time does she believe she should be doing something else with her life.

Today's workout is a ladder interval set—not very scientific, really, and not what her coach would tell her to do. But one workout a week, she follows her own instructions instead of her coach's. This workout is one lap hard, one lap easy, two laps hard, two laps easy, three laps hard, three laps easy, all the way up to six and then back down. She's been doing this ladder workout for years, every Tuesday, and it's always brutal.

On the first hard lap, which is always the toughest, everything hurts, but she rams through it, opening up her lungs and getting her legs used to the sting, then she eases up and pedals easily through her off laps. When she ramps into the two-lap hard section, her mind drifts to something that happened at work today. One of the trucks broke down in central Missouri and was going to be at least 10 hours late to its destination in Tulsa, Oklahoma. The customer was pissed, too, sending her a number of nasty e-mails, followed by a lengthy and incredibly nasty phone call in which the customer was screaming at her and telling her she may be the worst logistics coordinator in the entire country! Heidi remained calm. She absorbed the insults. She assured the customer the truck would get there within a reasonable time frame, and the customer hung up.

Now she digs deep and pushes out of the saddle and focuses all the strength she's developed in the gym into powering her bike forward. She feels like she is floating over the track and going faster and faster, and if she were to search through her brain for any trace of her job, she wouldn't find it.

Tray *could have been* a track racer.

Everybody says that to him because they know he's really fast. Everybody says he should race in the Alley Cat races downtown, too. They say he'd win by huge margins! But Tray doesn't give a rat's ass about official measures of speed. He does like his track bike a lot, but he's using it to make a living. He's delivering envelopes and packages and legal documents and the like from one office building to the next.

On this particular trip, he's delivering 10 submarine sandwiches to a law office.

He has the sandwiches placed carefully in his messenger bag, and the bag rests as comfortably on his back as a baby would rest in a crib. He doesn't know exactly the speed he's traveling along the street, but he's keeping up with the traffic, no problem. At one stoplight, he executes a track stand so perfect that he amazes himself. Ah, the joy!

At the law office, he locks his bike on a light pole, goes inside into the insane air-conditioning, and stands before the receptionist's desk.

——————— the Messenger: TRAY ———————

1. Lean racer's build.
2. Eyes hyperalert for whatever may appear on the road ahead.
3. Helmet, sign of wisdom.

She's old—like, really old, like in-her-sixties old—and doesn't appreciate the look of him one bit. A black kid with dreadlocks? In a law office? She stares at him as if he has been sent to drag her off somewhere remote and keep her hostage for the rest of her life. She can't seem to speak.

Tray's used to the looks, so he keeps the situation on task. He says, "Delivery." He reaches into his bag and produces a wrapped sandwich. She freezes. "It's a sandwich, ma'am." But he skips saying, "Not a gun." "The office ordered these sandwiches."

"Oh," the lady says. "Of course." She rises and tells him she'll be right back and then disappears down a hallway.

Meantime, Tray places all 10 wrapped sandwiches on the receptionist's desk and gets his confirmation paperwork ready for signature.

Now the receptionist returns with a tall, lean white guy in a shirt and tie. The guy says, "So *you're* the bike delivery guy." A statement, not a question.

Tray confirms that he is.

"I'm a rider, too—though I don't deliver anything. I do some racing, from time to time."

Tray gives the guy a big grin and doesn't pursue the subject of bike racing, because he prefers to keep things on a business level with people when he's on delivery. He says, "Sign for delivery?"

The guy signs and says, "You know, that's really cool you can ride a bike for a living. I wish I could do that." Then the guy puts a 10-dollar bill in Tray's hand and pats him on the back.

"Thanks, man," Tray says. "Gotta run now."

Outside, Tray unlocks his bike and gets ready to mount up. He sees, a few feet away, a skinny white hipster kid with red Chuck Taylors and skinny jeans and a striped long-sleeved T-shirt standing next to a bright-red fixie bike with bright-red rims. The kid is staring at Tray as if waiting for a comment.

Tray knows what the hipster wants to hear. He says, "Cool bike."

The kid says, "It certainly is."

Tray's bike is plain, with regular unpainted aluminum rims, which he likes because he doesn't want to *look* at his bike, he wants to *ride* his bike.

Tray nods at the kid—who doesn't really react—then jumps on his bike and books down the street to pick up his next delivery.

Jason watches the dude in dreads riding off on his *lame fixie.*

That guy's bike has no sense of flair whatsoever—just a bike, nothing more.

Now Jason's friend Derrick comes pushing his bike around the corner from the coffee shop. Derrick's bike is really awesome—lime-green rims and a flat-black frame. In black light, you'd only see the wheels, which would be trippy indeed.

Derrick digs a pack of cigarettes out of his skinny-jean pocket, taps out two smokes, and gives one to Jason. They both light up and lean against their bikes and blow simultaneous funnels of smoke toward the sky.

Jason says, "You shoulda seen this dude on a fixie a minute ago."

Derrick asks, "Who was it?"

"I don't know. A dude with no clue. I mean, if you're gonna get a

---

the Hipster: JASON

1. Classic cycling cap promoting components that aren't on his bike.
2. Cigarette.
3. Tats, meant to make nonbadass arms look badass.
4. Chuck Taylors, perhaps the world's worst cycling shoes.

fixie, you need to turn on the style just a little, show you care."

Derrick drags long off his cigarette and exhales through his nose. Smoke washes over him like a tired wave over a slacker beach. "You ever see the guy at the Alley Cat?"

"Nope." Jason chuckles some smoke out. "Totally had the I'm-a-bike-messenger vibe working, too. Like anyone with a messenger bag is supposed to be the real deal!"

"Totally. See my bag, people! Ain't it cool?" Derrick outstretches his arms in a form of dismissive crucifixion.

"Even more pathetic: The guy's messenger bag was from L.L. Bean."

Derrick says, "Maybe his mom bought it for him for Christmas."

They have a deluxe laugh about this and take a few more drags on their smokes and then toe the butts on the sidewalk.

Jason asks, "Where to?"

"To Rummy's house?"

Jason agrees and takes his Campagnolo cycling cap from his back pocket and places it on his head. Once Derrick's done the same, they get on their bikes and roll on the sidewalk off into the very hip, very styling distance.

Fixed Gear Cyclists

True enough, fixies are currently the *trend du jour* among young skinny hipsters—or maybe the trend is already over and those ultragroovy urban skinny kids have moved on to the next thing that *turns the crank* of their youthful hearts.

It really doesn't matter. Once the photo ops have gone away and the kids have gone away and adopted a new style of clothing and hair and so forth, fixed-geared riding will still be there, stoically carrying on the way it always has: on velodromes, on delivery bikes, and of course on single-speed mountain bikes and cyclocross bikes.

Fixie riding, in fact, is the original form of cycling—the idea being you have one gear, and if you want to stop your bike, you pedal backward. This is so simple that, yes, even 2-year-olds on tricycles can do it! The fixie's place in the pantheon of Bike Tribes, however, is difficult to pin down precisely on account of the wide range of fixies and because certain aspects of fixie cycling simply aren't available everywhere. Not every community has a velodrome, which is a shame, but the consequence of this is that track racers are spread out in a few cities around the country, and most cyclists have never been on a track and have never seen a track except on TV. The same is true of bicycle messengers. Most cities don't have bicycle messengers, and for certain, if you live in a small town, you will never see a bicycle messenger.

The real fixie rider, therefore, is a person of mystery to most people in cycling, and because of this, everybody thinks fixies are cool. If more people rode fixies, this coolness would probably not be so cool anymore.

WHAT VINTAGE DO YOU PREFER?

Brian and Anne *love* riding their bikes to the art openings at the gallery downtown, usually a couple, three times a month.

They think it makes an excellent statement, as a couple, that they are not driving their boring Volvo to the art opening but instead are arriving on human-powered pieces of art at a place where people appreciate pieces of art. And tonight's bikes are just perfect. Matching men's and women's 1967 Schwinn Collegiates. Brian bought them for cheap off eBay about a year ago and completely restored them with original parts, even the chains, meaning the only items not authentic on these bikes are the tires and inner tubes.

_____ the Vintage Riders: BRIAN and ANNE _____

1. They hope people are watching them.

2. Bikes look like they have been teleported from the 1960s.

Brian and Anne are dressed to match the bikes, too—Brian in his corduroy pants and sweater and RFK-style glasses, and Anne in her plaid skirt and white shirt, hair pulled back in a vintage bun, cat's-eye glasses, naturally, and bright red lipstick. So when they roll up to the gallery, they look about as Norman Rockwell as a couple in their midthirties possibly could.

They step off their bikes and stand next to them looking very proud. There's art in the gallery, of course—their friend Jesse is having a show tonight—but there's no need to rush inside.

"Well," Anne says, "where is everybody?"

Brian looks around. A few cars move up and down the street. Inside the gallery, a few people are mingling around the art and around the snack table.

Brian says, "They're inside."

Anne asks, "We don't have to go in yet, do we?"

They linger for a while, hoping somebody will ask them about their bikes, and eventually they're in luck. Big Ed himself, from Big Ed's Cyclery, comes walking up the sidewalk with his wife, Cheryl. They're in shorts and T-shirts and have their usual air of hippie mellowness about them.

Brian asks, "Ed, what are you doing here?"

Ed says, "We're gonna check out Jesse's art show, of course." Ed looks at the matching bikes and nods and smokes. "Tell you what, Brian, you always have the coolest bikes. How long it take you to rebuild these?"

Anne says, "Brian spent almost a year on these."

Ed says, "Looks like it's worth it. Wow."

Then Ed excuses himself and goes inside the gallery with his wife to see the show.

Brian and Anne smile at each other now. "Did you hear that?" Brian asks. "Big Ed digs our bikes!"

Anne is so happy her cheeks flush. "I love our old bikes, Brian."

Brian gives her a big kiss and a hug. "And I love you, baby."

They lean their bikes against the gallery's outside wall, lock them together, and walk into the gallery holding hands.

The Vintage Bike Rider

The *most important* item to note about the rider
of vintage bicycles—we're talking the authentic
rider/collector here—is that this person views
bikes the way people used to eat Lay's potato chips,
which is to say you *never* can have just one.

Because of this, the vintage bicycle enthusiast is almost never a person living in a tiny apartment. The vintage bike person needs room to spread out, and sometimes a normal garage just isn't enough room for the bikes, not to mention the vintage parts and wheels and clothing and God only knows what else a person can find on eBay or on various cycling message boards throughout the world! Ideally, the vintage bike collector would have a large outbuilding on a spacious property with, of course, plenty of room in the driveway to test out the bikes during the restoration process.

For clarification, then, when we refer to a vintage bicycle collector, we don't mean the old drunk who's lost his driver's license and gets around town on a brown 1979 Schwinn Continental with the handlebar flipped upside-right. Now, that *is* a vintage bike, and the old drunk is a vintage in and of himself. But by "vintage," we mean a bicycle of a certain age that has been either maintained excellently or rebuilt to roll the way it was originally intended to roll, which is at a level of magnificence, of course.

There is an element of retro art to the vintage bike community, too, and maybe vintage bike collectors are a healthier, more environmentally friendly version of people who are in vintage automobile clubs. It's hard for anybody—cyclist or noncyclist—to take issue with things from the past that are maintained close to their original condition. If you give a person my age, for instance, an old View-Master that still works (for those of you who are still young, this was a little plastic 3-D picture-viewer device that was very popular with children in the late 1960s), that person will be more than delighted to see it! It's nostalgia, for sure, which is something the snarky among us don't appreciate. But then again, in the cycling world, we love bikes of almost any kind, and when we see the vintage bikes rolling on the street, we can't help but feel happy because we are seeing the history of the thing we love. No member of any Bike Tribe feels bad when they see an old bike in good shape.

BEACH CRUISERS

Tracy and Pam have it made on the bike path along the river today. *Beach cruisers. Sunshine.*

Not too hot, not too windy. Flip-flops and shorts and bikini tops. Is this not perfection?

Tracy is blonde and tall, and when she pedals, her cruiser rocks gently from side to side; her torso and back bob back and forth with each pushing-down on the pedals. Pam is brunette and holds considerably more still on her bike. They are both sitting upright, with their hair flowing behind them and their wide sunglasses reflecting a steady glint of the sun.

Tracy asks, "You think it's weird we're riding beach cruisers when there is no beach?"

Pam ponders this and pulls her lower lip under her front teeth. "Is

---

the Beach Cruisers: TRACY and PAM

1. Sunglasses. Strain on the eyes will ruin the vibe.
2. Upright position. Mellow speed. Why hurry?

it weird to ride a mountain bike when there is no mountain?"

They burst out laughing.

Tracy says, "You're not going to start up with the thing about does a one-legged duck swim in circles, are you?"

"Not till we get to the bar."

Pam clears her throat and becomes more serious. "Here's a question: You think we look stupid riding bikes like this?"

Tracy says, "Who gives a shit? I'm triple-clicking 'Like' this on Facebook."

"Smart-ass," Pam says.

They both sigh in a happy way. This is truly great. They get to ride beach cruisers on the path in the sun, then they'll have drinks on the patio with all their friends at Quint's Riverfront.

Tracy says, "I'm thinking I'd like to accessorize."

"With what?"

"A basket." Tracy reaches one hand over the handlebar and makes a gesture in the shape of a basket. As she's doing this, her bike wobbles, and she has to steady it with both hands on the bar.

Pam says, "You could carry a huge purse in there."

"Or a cooler!"

"Or a Chihuahua!"

Tracy can't stop laughing. "That's what these bikes are made for—transporting Chihuahuas."

They keep laughing and pedaling and talking about other little dogs they could take with them on their beach cruisers, and when they arrive at the Quint's Riverfront deck, they're still laughing. Lots of people are here today, too, under cabana tables and totally relaxing with drinks on this excellent afternoon.

The Beach Cruisers

Somewhere in the world of cycling, amidst all the
intensity and people driven to achieve something
specific—an exercise goal, a weight-loss goal,

a victory in a road race, a 32nd-place finish in a Masters cyclocross race,
et cetera—there has to be a place where nothing really matters other than
mellowness and taking it easy and redefining the art of chill even on the
sunniest days of summer. Beach cruisers are what we all need, maybe,
when our life on bicycles starts to wear us down and make us feel like
we're in a two-wheeled rut from which there will be no climbing out.

Serious cyclists almost uniformly poke fun at people riding beach
cruisers because they're going too slow and they're not showing any level
of dedication to cycling and, perhaps the worst, the people who ride
beach cruisers don't really think of themselves as part of the Bike Tribes.
They're just doing their thing and not worrying too much about how
they fit in to the larger context of cycling. They're certainly not going to
get into a shouting match with somebody about the proper way to ride
in a paceline or the best form of community cycling activism. No way.
All of that stops with the beach cruiser. Serious cyclists, if they have one
problem above all other problems, often don't respect people on bikes
who don't take what they're doing seriously.

Maybe what we should all do one of these days is put a boom box in
the basket of a beach cruiser and head out on a nice flat bike path and
pedal so effortlessly that we don't break the faintest hint of a sweat. And
when people wave to us and tell us we're groovy, we can say, "Yeah, we
most certainly are."

TOGETHER

In one little town, where all the people involved in
cycling bring their business to *two bike shops,* or
maybe only *one bike shop . . .*

where the sum of people who would gladly identify themselves as
cyclists may not exceed 200, there will never come a time when everybody comes together on their bicycles and points somewhere east or
west or north or south and rides together in harmony till they get there.
This is sad, l guess, but inevitable. The bikes are different—built for different situations and different terrain—and the riders are different in
their motivations and their dreams and the reasons they want to balance their bodies on a machine with two wheels and propel it forward
with two legs. Maybe it's too easy to say we're all alike because of two
wheels and because of pedals and tires and chains and how there's
something about that miracle of staying upright on a bicycle that tran-
scends the activity that cycling is and allows it to become the way of life
that most of us would like it to be. Maybe it's too easy to lump us all
together.

The Olympics come to mind. There, athletes compete in who knows
how many sports, but the chances of these athletes having connections

with each other during their training lives—bobsledders with figure skaters, boxers with archers, ski jumpers with hockey players—are about the same as permanent world peace breaking out tomorrow morning. Yet at the opening ceremony of the Olympics, they come together in one place, with one purpose, which is to engage in a fair athletic endeavor wherein the strongest and fastest and most nimble person will be declared the winner. They are athletes. This makes them similar human beings. This means they should be capable of understanding all the fellowship and kindness and love that comes with being similar human beings.

Maybe someday, when the world is finally a perfect place, when people don't find ways to become irritated over their differences, cyclists will come together in total harmony and decide that maybe the best thing for us to do is acknowledge that we're just doing the same thing. We're really just pedaling.